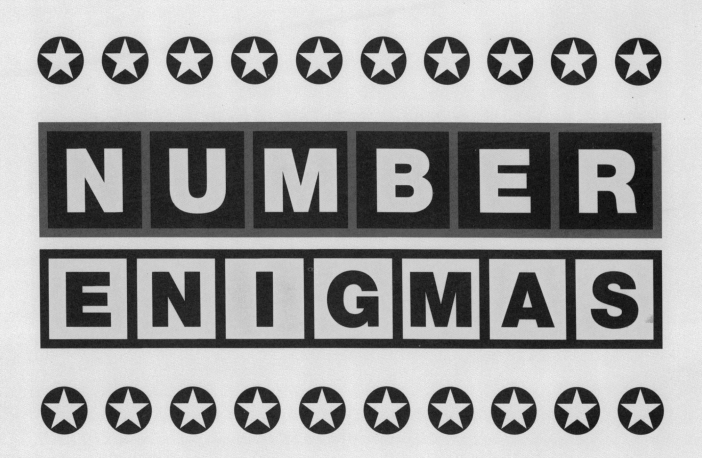

NUMBER ENIGMAS

THUNDER BAY
P·R·E·S·S
San Diego, California

Thunder Bay Press

An imprint of the Advantage Publishers Group

5880 Oberlin Drive, San Diego, CA 92121-4794

www.thunderbaybooks.com

Published by arrangement with Book Creation Ltd., London, and Book Creation, LLC, New York.

All puzzles, artwork, and text copyright © 2003 Book Creation Ltd.

All notations of errors or omissions should be addressed to Thunder Bay Press, Editorial Department, at the above address. All other correspondence (author inquiries, permissions) concerning the content of this book should be addressed to Book Creation Ltd., 20 Lochaline Street, London W6 9SH, United Kingdom; E-mail: info@librios.com

ISBN 1–59223–018–0

Printed and bound in China

2 3 4 5   09 08 07 06 05

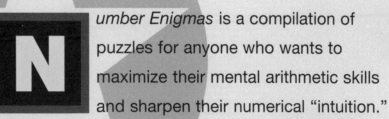

umber Enigmas is a compilation of puzzles for anyone who wants to maximize their mental arithmetic skills and sharpen their numerical "intuition." No matter what your level of ability, a carefully graded series of challenges ensures that this book will have plenty for you.

The relationship between words and numbers is curious—words and numbers are both handled by the left hemisphere of the human brain and processed in the same way, regardless of their seeming differences. There are ten digits and twenty-six letters, yet numbers are infinite while the variety of words is finite. In spite of the fact that number puzzles use only ten digits along with the four basic mathematical operations (and perhaps the occasional square root or two), there is an amazing variety to be found in the world of number puzzles. Before you know it, you'll be completing sequences in a flash, dashing through the most difficult divisions, and scaling the heights of our number pyramids. Traditional formats for word-based puzzles, such as crosswords and word searches, also get their own numeric treatments.

Each puzzle in *Number Enigmas* has been carefully graded according to a ten-star system—the more stars there are, the harder that puzzle will be. Remember that these ratings are based on an average performance, so don't be surprised if you breeze through a ten-star stumper (or are baffled by a three-star puzzler)! But it doesn't end there—since speed of calculation is just as important as accuracy, every challenge has been given its own time limit for you to work toward.

There are no sneaky tricks here. You don't need to know logarithms, calculus, or group theory (or even know what they mean). All of the puzzles are based on straightforward operations, although some are better disguised than others. If you find that you can't crunch through a particular calculation, the answers section at the back of the book will provide you with the solution. Every question in the book has been numbered—simply refer to the same number in the answers section and all will be revealed. But have one last attempt at solving the problem before resorting to the solutions, since the satisfaction of cracking a seemingly impossible problem is its own reward.

By the end of *Number Enigmas*, having honed your skills on these mathematical puzzles, you'll find yourself seeing numerical relationships and solving mathematical problems more quickly and easily than you ever imagined ✪

—Alison Moore

1 DIFFICULTY ✪✪✪✪✪✩✩✩✩✩

Target time: 5 minutes

Can you place the tiles in the grid so that:

* each row and column contains two squares of each color, and

* each row and column contains exactly one of each number?

2 DIFFICULTY ✪✪✪✪✩✩✩✩✩✩
Target time: 8 minutes

Can you fit these numbers into the grid? One number has already been inserted to help you get started.

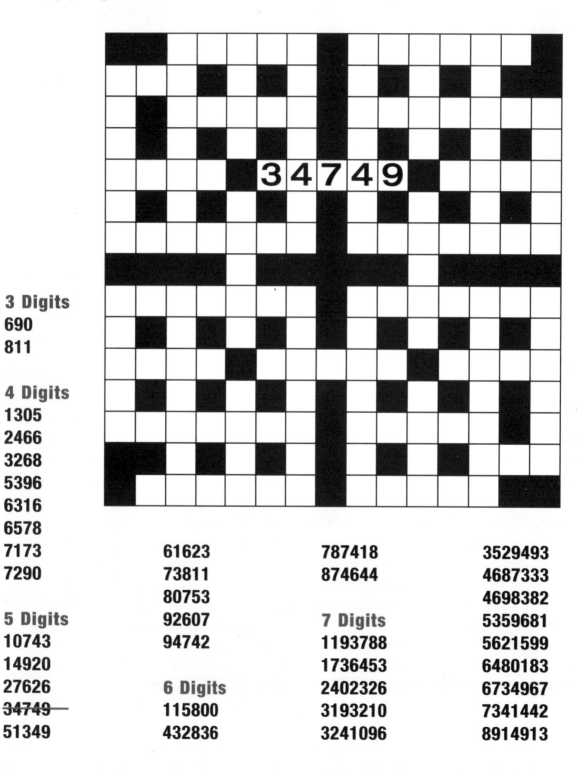

3 Digits
690
811

4 Digits
1305
2466
3268
5396
6316
6578
7173
7290

5 Digits
10743
14920
27626
~~34749~~
51349

61623
73811
80753
92607
94742

6 Digits
115800
432836

787418
874644

7 Digits
1193788
1736453
2402326
3193210
3241096

3529493
4687333
4698382
5359681
5621599
6480183
6734967
7341442
8914913

3 DIFFICULTY ✪✪✪✪✪✪✪✪✪✪
Target time: 3 minutes

Make a calculation totaling the figure on the right, and using some or all of the numbers on the left with any of the four standard mathematical operators (+, −, x, and ÷).

3, 4, 5, 8, 9, 25 = 527

4 DIFFICULTY ✪✪✪✪✪✪✪✪✪✪
Target time: 5 minutes

Study these balloons carefully for one minute, then answer the questions on page 10 without checking back.

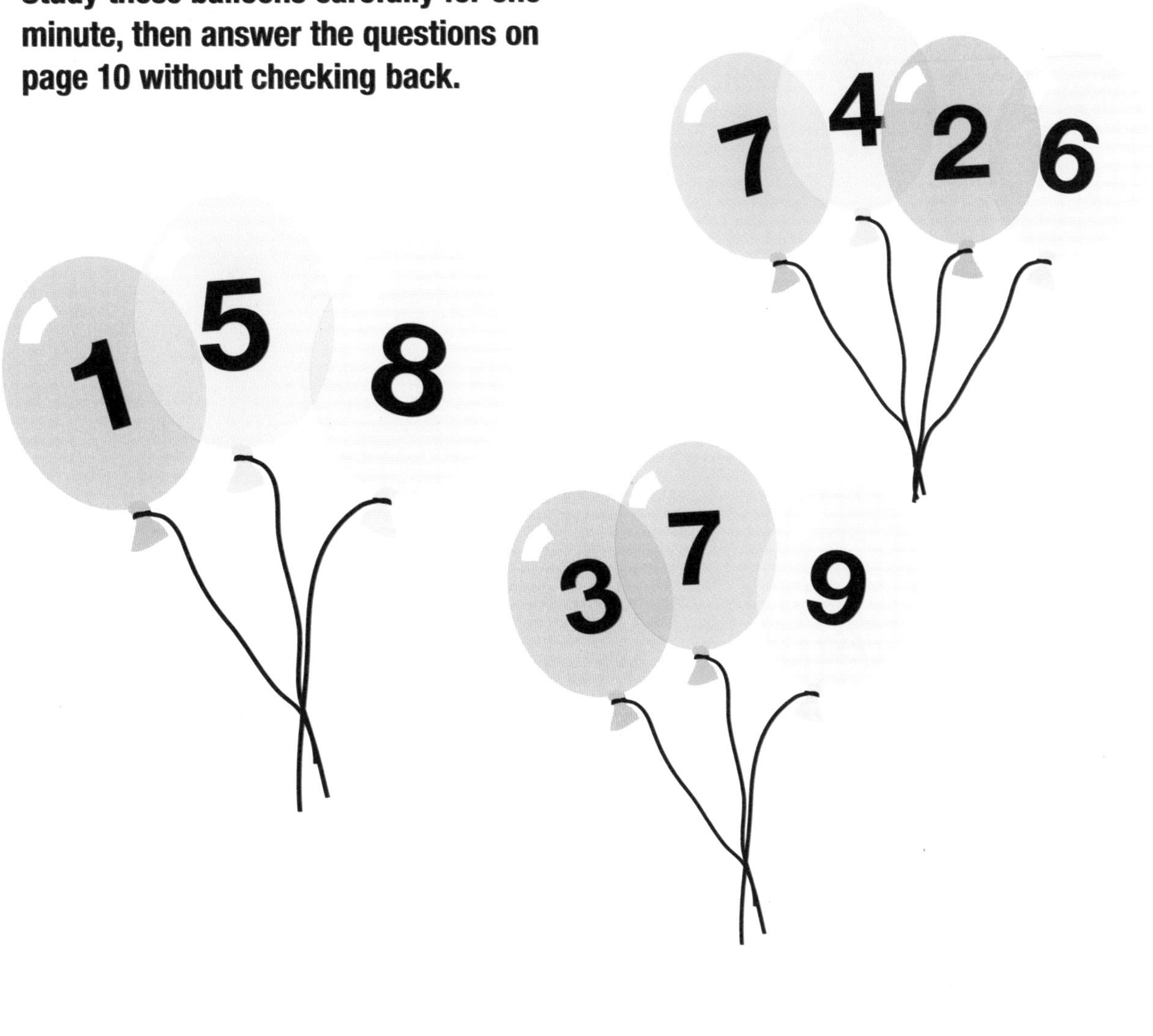

7 4 2 6

1 5 8

3 7 9

[4] DIFFICULTY ✪✪✪✪✪✪✪✪✪✪

Target time: 5 minutes

Can you answer these questions about the puzzle on page 9 without checking back?

1. The numbers on two bunches of balloons add up to the same figure. What is it?

2. What's the total of the numbers on the pink balloons?

3. Which number appears twice?

4. On which colored balloons does it appear?

5. How many pink balloons have odd numbers?

6. Which odd number appears on a blue balloon?

7. Which even number appears on a yellow balloon?

8. How many balloons are green?

5 DIFFICULTY ✪✪✪✪✪✪✪✪✪✪

Target time: 3 minutes

Which clock face is the odd one out?

a   b   c   d

6 DIFFICULTY ○○○○○○○○○○○
Target time: 10 minutes

Starting with the yellow square on the top left corner, find the path through the squares, calculating each step to lead you to the solution on the bottom right corner. You may not pass through the same square more than once.

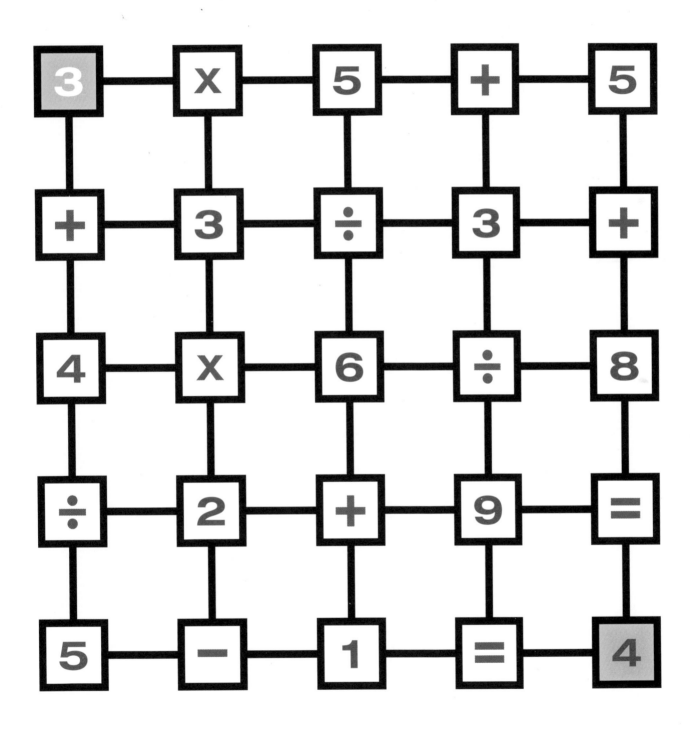

7 DIFFICULTY ✪✪✪✪✪✪✪✪✪
Target time: 3 minutes

Consider the apples, bananas, and oranges shown below. Given that scales a and b balance perfectly, how many apples are needed to balance scale c?

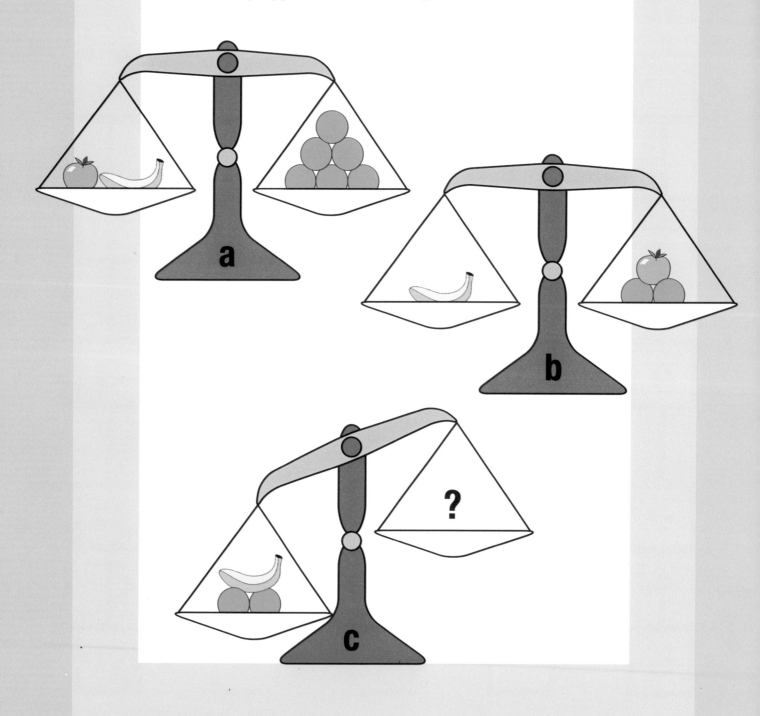

8 DIFFICULTY ⊛⊛⊛⊛⊛⊛⊛⊛⊛⊛

Target time: 8 minutes

Find the solutions to the following calculations in the grid, reading up, down, backward, forward, and diagonally!

1. 9 x 9 x 9 x 9
2. (40 x 40) + 400
3. (100 – 44) x 22
4. 8,989 + 1,111
5. 77 + 88 + 88 + 99
6. 1,234 x 5
7. 44 x 66

8. 666 + 334
9. 8,765 – 1,111
10. (9 + 9) x 99
11. (10,000 ÷ 20) + 20
12. 90,990 ÷ 3
13. (565 x 2) x 2

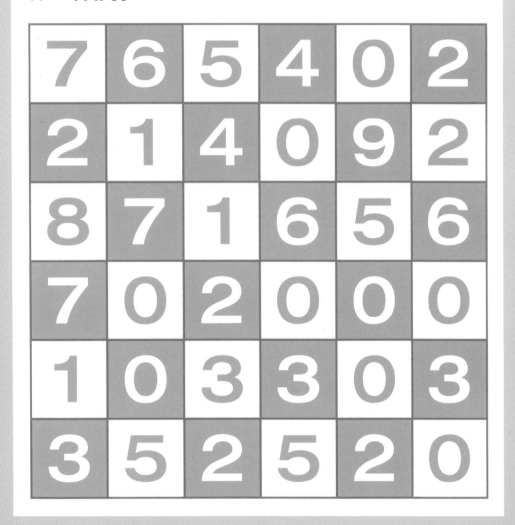

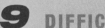 **DIFFICULTY** ✪✪✪✪✩✩✩✩✩✩

Target time: 6 minutes

Every row and column contains the same numbers and signs, but they are arranged in a different order each time. Find the correct order to arrive at the final totals shown.

3	**+**	**2**	**x**	**6**	**−**	**5**	**= 25**
						=	**17**
						=	**27**
						=	**24**
=		**=**		**=**		**=**	
21		**7**		**9**		**15**	

10 DIFFICULTY ✪✪✪✪✪✩✩✩✩✩

Target time: 5 minutes

This is a two-player game. Players take turns removing as many coins as they like from one of the three rows. If you pick up the last coin, you lose the game. Once you've played the game a few times, see if you can work out how to guarantee a win by starting first.

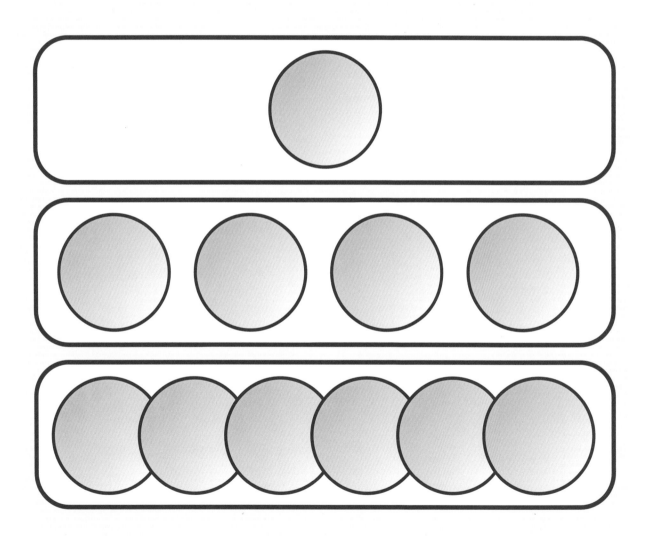

11 DIFFICULTY ✪✪✪✪✰✰✰✰✰✰

Target time: 4 minutes

The number 543,789 appears just once in this grid and occurs in a straight line, running either backward or forward in a horizontal, vertical, or diagonal direction. Can you locate it?

5	4	3	7	9	8	7	3	5	4	9	5
9	8	3	5	9	3	7	5	3	4	8	4
3	4	7	5	4	3	5	9	5	3	7	7
4	5	4	9	4	5	8	4	7	3	9	3
5	4	3	7	9	3	3	8	5	9	8	8
9	3	4	8	5	7	9	9	4	9	9	9
4	7	9	4	9	8	9	7	7	3	4	5
8	5	9	5	4	3	5	8	9	8	8	3
7	9	5	3	5	9	8	7	3	4	5	9
5	1	4	7	4	8	7	5	9	7	5	3
8	5	3	5	3	3	4	9	5	8	4	4
9	8	7	3	5	4	5	4	3	9	7	8

12 DIFFICULTY ✪✪✪✪✪✪✪✪✪✪
Target time: 10 minutes

Can you fit these numbers into the grid? One number has already been inserted to help you get started.

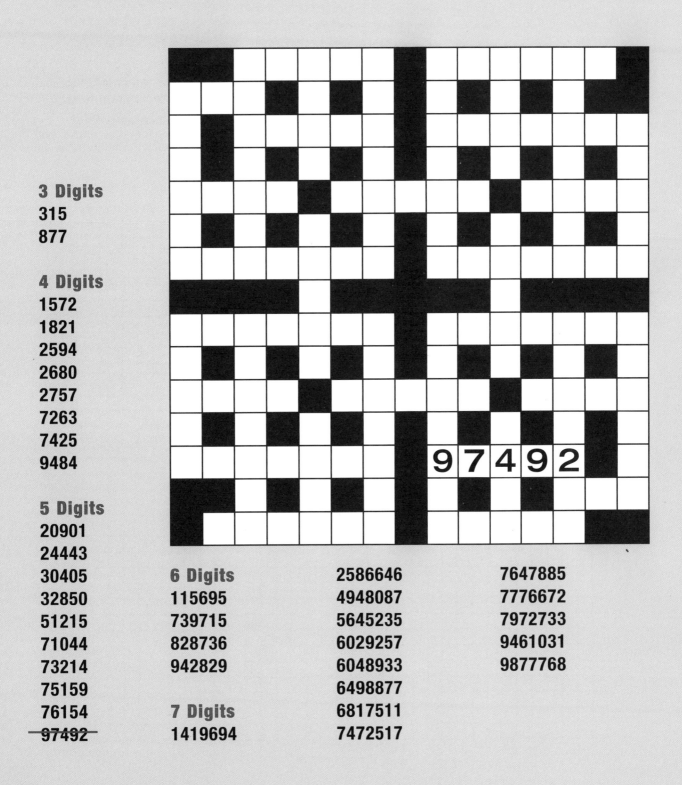

3 Digits
315
877

4 Digits
1572
1821
2594
2680
2757
7263
7425
9484

5 Digits
20901
24443
30405
32850
51215
71044
73214
75159
76154
97492

6 Digits
115695
739715
828736
942829

7 Digits
1419694

2586646
4948087
5645235
6029257
6048933
6498877
6817511
7472517

7647885
7776672
7972733
9461031
9877768

13 DIFFICULTY ✪✪✪✪✪✪✪✪✪✪

Target time: 30 minutes

If you like nonograms, this one should suit you!

HOW TO DO A NONOGRAM:

Along each row or column there are numbers that indicate how many blocks of black squares are in a line.
For example, "3, 4, 5" indicates that from left to right or top to bottom, there is a group of three black squares, then a group of four black squares, then another group of five black squares.

Each block of black squares on the same line must have at least one white square between it and the next block of black squares. Blocks of black squares may or may not have a number of white squares before and after them.

It is sometimes possible to determine which squares will be black without reference to other lines or columns.
It is helpful to put a small dot in a square you know will be empty.

Column clues (top to bottom):

```
                                              2 4     4 2
            2 3       3 2                     3 1     1 3
    3 2 1 1 3 2 5 2 3 1 1 2 3       1 3 5 5 1 2 13 2 1 5 5 3 1
    7 6 5 4 8 9 1 9 8 4 5 6 7       7 6 5 4 3 2 1 2 3 4 5 6 7
 15 4 6 7 8 1 2 13 2 1 8 7 6 4 15 15 7 6 5 4 3 2 1 2 3 4 5 6 7 15
```

Row clues (top to bottom):

```
                15
        3 5 3   1
        2 3 2   3
        1 1 1   5
        1 1 1   5
          1 1   3
    1 1 2 1     2
    1 1 4 1     4
          2 2   13
    3 3 4 1     4
    4 4 2 1     2
        5 5     1
        6 6     3
        7 7     5
                15
                15
        1 7     7
        3 6     6
        5 5     5
        7 4     4
        9 3     3
      11 2      2
      13 1      1
      13 2      2
      13 3      3
      13 4      4
    3 1 3 5     5
        3 6     6
        5 7     7
                15
```

14 DIFFICULTY ✪✪✪✪✪✪✪✪✪✪

Target time: 4 minutes

Each block is equal to the sum of the two numbers beneath it. Find all the missing numbers.

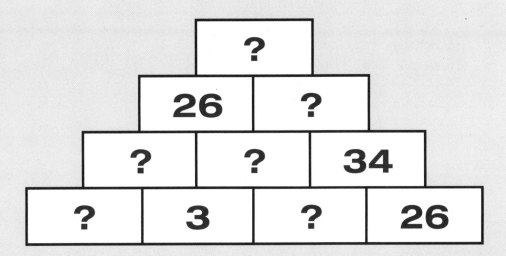

15 DIFFICULTY ✪✪✪✪✪✪✪✪✪✪

Target time: 4 minutes

These four points are the corners of a square. If a has coordinates of (4, 5), and c is at (10, 1), what are the coordinates of b and d?

16 DIFFICULTY ✪✪✪✪✩✩✩✩✩✩

Target time: 3 minutes

Which is the odd number out?

159, 367, 589, 258, 486, 679

17 DIFFICULTY ✪✪✪✩✩✩✩✩✩✩

Target time: 4 minutes

Replace the question marks with mathematical symbols to produce the correct answer. Only the four basic operators (+, −, x, and ÷) are permitted. Perform calculations in strict left to right order. Can you find two possible solutions?

6 ? 2 ? 2 ? 3 ? 7

= 16

18 DIFFICULTY ✪✪✪✪✩✩✩✩✩✩
Target time: 4 minutes

Can you place the tiles in the grid so that:

★ each row and column contains two squares of each color, and
★ no row or column contains more than one of any number?

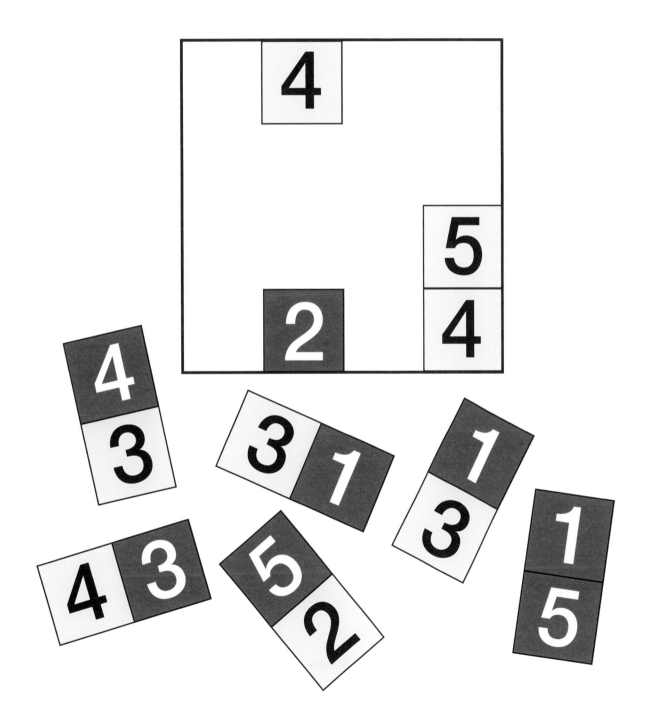

19 DIFFICULTY ✪✪✪✪✩✩✩✩✩✩
Target time: 3 minutes

Place a number in the middle box that divides into all the other numbers without leaving a remainder. The answer is greater than 1.

273		126
231		168
147		252

20 DIFFICULTY ✪✪✪✪✩✩✩✩✩✩
Target time: 3 minutes

At a local club, a dice game is played that involves throwing two dice and betting a stake of $5. What are the rules, and how much did Gary Gambler win or lose when he threw a 5, followed by a 2? Study the clues below to discover the answer!

1. Gina threw a 4, followed by a 4, and lost her whole stake. She paid another stake and tried again. This time she threw a 3, followed by a 1, and got $6 back, thus winning $1 on her second try.

2. George threw a 6, followed by a 2, and got $12 back, so won $7.

3. Grant threw a 1, followed by a 3, and got $6 back, so won $1.

21 DIFFICULTY ✪✪✪✪✪✪✪✪✪✪

Target time: 5 minutes

Given that scales a and b balance perfectly, how many suns are needed to balance scale c?

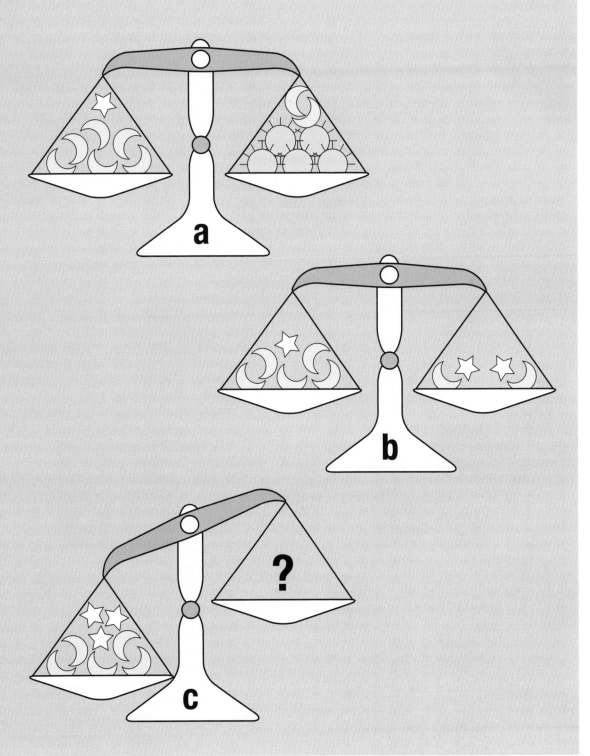

22 DIFFICULTY

Target time: 3 minutes

What number should replace the question mark in the following sequence?

100, 98.75, 96.25, 95, 92.5, ?

23 DIFFICULTY

Target time: 4 minutes

Find out the mystery sequence hidden in the dominoes, then decide which number should replace the question mark.

 a = 34

 b = 51

 c = 71

 d = ?

24 DIFFICULTY ✪✪✪✪✪✪✪✪✪

Target time: 6 minutes

Can you divide this square into four equally shaped parts of nine smaller squares, each containing two different numbers and two different shapes?

25 DIFFICULTY ✪✪✪✪✪✪✪✪✪✪

Target time: 8 minutes

And now can you divide this square into four identical shapes, each composed of sixteen squares, and each containing four different numbers?

26 DIFFICULTY ✪✪✪✪✩✩✩✩✩✩
Target time: 4 minutes

Which domino (a, b, c, or d) should fill the empty space?

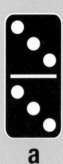  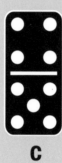 

a   b   c   d

27 DIFFICULTY ✪✪✪✪✩✩✩✩✩✩
Target time: 3 minutes

Place a number in the middle box that divides into all the other numbers without leaving a remainder. The answer is greater than 1.

102		442
136		561
187		306

28 DIFFICULTY ✪✪✪✪✪✫✫✫✫✫
Target time: 5 minutes

**Each block is equal to the sum of the two numbers beneath it.
Find all the missing numbers.**

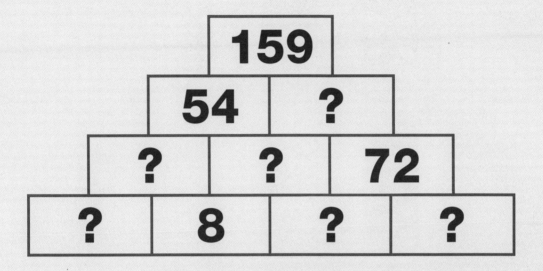

29 DIFFICULTY ✪✪✪✪✫✫✫✫✫✫
Target time: 3 minutes

Which is the odd number out?

1,235   2,134

3,145   4,268

5,279   4,569

30 DIFFICULTY ✪✪✪✪✪✪✪✪✪✪

Target time: 3 minutes

What time should come next on clock e?

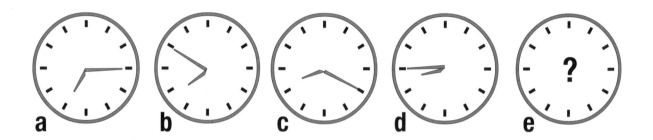

a   b   c   d   e

31 DIFFICULTY ✪✪✪✪✪✪✪✪✪✪

Target time: 4 minutes

Replace the question marks with mathematical symbols to produce the correct answer. Only the four basic operators (+, −, x, and ÷) are permitted. Perform calculations in strict left to right order. Can you find two possible solutions?

12 ? 4 ? 7
? 8 = 7

32 DIFFICULTY ✪✪✪✪☆☆☆☆☆☆

Target time: 6 minutes

Can you fit these numbers into the grid? One number has already been given to help you get started.

3 Digits
544
675

4 Digits
2534
3145
4812
4983
5343
6911
7403
9462

5 Digits
20010
~~35041~~
46255
57193
57488

69606
74366
81587
87449
92579

6 Digits
379253
681202

813024
916115

7 Digits
1712470
2041019
3496883
3756076
4099359

4109509
4549428
5179153
6015117
7810067
7895619
8107408
8589334
9264533

33 DIFFICULTY ✪✪✪✪✪✪✪✩✩✩
Target time: 5 minutes

Weigh up the symbols below. Given that scales a and b balance perfectly, how many clubs are needed to balance scale c?

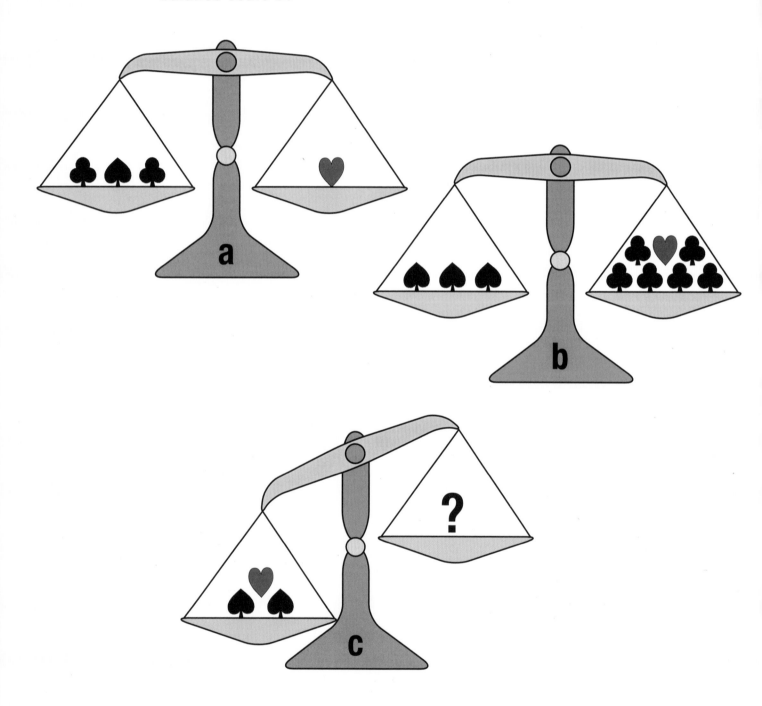

34 DIFFICULTY ✪✪✪✪✪✪✪✪✪✪
Target time: 3 minutes

Which number is the odd one out?

17   37   61
23   42   59

35 DIFFICULTY ✪✪✪✪✪✪✪✪✪✪
Target time: 3 minutes

At the local club, a dice game is played that involves throwing two dice and betting a stake of $12. What are the rules—and how much did Gary Gambler win or lose when he threw a 4, followed by a 5? Study the clues below to discover the answer!

1. Gina threw a 2, followed by a 2, and got $4 back, losing $8.

2. George threw a 6, followed by a 2, and broke even, so got $12 back.

3. Grant threw a 1, followed by a 3, and got $3 back, so lost $9.

36 DIFFICULTY ✪✪✪✪✪✰✰✰✰✰

Target time: 8 minutes

Find the answers to the following calculations in the grid, reading up, down, backward, forward, and diagonally.

1. 54,321 – 12,345
2. 15 x 15 x 15
3. 909 + 707
4. 55,000 ÷ 25
5. 11,111 + 12,345
6. 2,727 ÷ 9
7. (6,204 ÷ 2) ÷ 2
8. 10,000 – 4,445
9. 3,108 ÷ 7
10. 5 x 5 x 5 x 5 x 5
11. 15 x 51
12. 999 – 343

2	2	0	0	4	4
3	0	3	1	4	7
6	5	9	4	6	5
1	7	1	5	5	1
6	3	6	5	6	6
1	3	5	2	1	3

37 DIFFICULTY ✪✪✪✪✪✪✰✰✰✰

Target time: 4 minutes

Study these shapes for one minute, then see if you can answer
the questions that follow on page 34 without checking back.

38 DIFFICULTY ✪✪✪✪✪✪✪✰✰✰

Target time: 6 minutes

What theorem do these two diagrams prove?

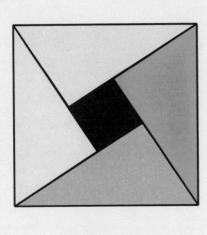

Fig. 1

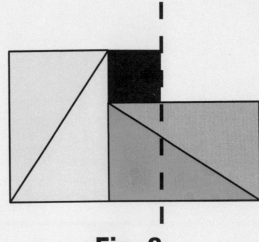

Fig. 2

[37] DIFFICULTY ✪✪✪✪✪✪✪✪✪✪

Target time: 4 minutes

Can you answer these questions about the puzzle on page 33 without checking back?

1. How many shapes have prime numbers?

2. Which two numbers will total a third number shown?

3. What is the total when you multiply the number on the blue shape by that on the pink shape?

4. Which shapes have odd numbers?

5. Which colors have even numbers?

6. What is the total reached by adding the number on the yellow shape to that on the square, then subtracting this total from the number on the shape on the far right?

39 DIFFICULTY ✪✪✪✪✪✪✪✪✪✪✪

Target time: 3 minutes

Make a calculation totaling the figure at the bottom using some or all of the numbers in the box with any of the four standard mathematical operators (+, −, x, and ÷).

4 ? 4 ? 6 ?

7 ? 9 ? 10

= 311

40 DIFFICULTY ✪✪✪✪✪✪✪✪✪✪
Target time: 6 minutes

The number 1,899,740 appears just once in this number-search grid and occurs in a straight line, running either backward or forward in a horizontal, vertical, or diagonal direction. Can you find it?

1	8	0	4	8	7	0	9	1	8	0	4
4	7	8	0	9	8	1	9	9	8	1	0
4	1	0	0	7	9	8	9	1	7	4	0
7	8	9	0	1	4	7	0	9	1	9	8
4	9	0	4	7	8	4	8	1	0	7	7
8	9	8	7	0	9	0	8	9	0	0	9
9	0	7	9	4	8	9	1	4	9	0	4
8	8	4	9	8	1	9	4	9	7	8	9
1	0	7	8	4	9	0	1	8	9	4	9
9	7	9	1	4	0	1	8	0	9	8	0
4	9	8	0	8	4	0	8	1	4	7	8
8	7	1	1	4	1	9	8	7	9	1	1

41 DIFFICULTY ✪✪✪✪✪✪✪☆☆

Target time: 8 minutes

Can you divide this square into four identical shapes, each composed of sixteen squares, and each containing four different numbers?

			3	3			
		1					
		1		2		1	1
				4	4	2	
2	2						3
	4						3
	4						

42 DIFFICULTY ✪✪✪✪✪✪✪✪☆☆

Target time: 6 minutes

Ten dominoes have been used to build this wall, but seven have been masked out. Can you place the missing dominoes correctly, bearing in mind that each vertical line of four numbers (as well as the two end vertical lines of two numbers) adds up to eight?

43 DIFFICULTY ★★★★☆☆☆☆☆☆

Target time: 3 minutes

Place a number in the middle box that divides into all the other numbers without leaving a remainder. The answer is greater than 1.

132		143
121		154
165		209

44 DIFFICULTY ★★★★★★☆☆☆☆

Target time: 3 minutes

Which of these is the odd number out?

17, 71, 88, 88, 176, 671, 846

45 DIFFICULTY ✪✪✪✪✪✪✪✪✪✪

Target time: 8 minutes

Traverse this maze from top to bottom (any entry point on the top row may be used). You may only move from a number divisible by 5 to one divisible by 6, from a number divisible by 6 to one divisible by 7, or from one divisible by 7 to one divisible by 5. You may not move diagonally.

66	14	18	65	26	55	19
77	50	21	16	49	24	63
75	33	37	78	40	54	10
96	98	96	25	18	15	36
31	20	36	49	54	50	56
98	48	11	23	91	72	56
20	28	45	78	91	15	72
12	23	54	77	85	95	21
16	25	24	66	14	91	40

46 DIFFICULTY ✪✪✪✪✪✪✪✪✪✪
Target time: 30 minutes

Nonograms make good games. You will be bowled over by this one.
(See page 18 for advice on how to complete a nonogram.)

Column clues (top):

					1		5	3	1			3	1	1				1	1										
1			1	5		1	1	1	1	5		8		1	3		2	3	12	2	2	12	3	3					
8	1	5		5	1	1	1	1	1	1	1	1	1	1	1	1	1	1	1	2	2	2	2	2	2	2	3		
1	1	1	1	1	1	1	1	1	4	1	3	7	1	1	1	1	1	1	1	2	2	2	2	2	2	2	3		
1	1	1	1	1	3	7	9	6	13	9	7	15	15	13	13	11	9	7	3	12	2	2	1	1	1	1	1	3	13

Row clues (left):

		1	1	2
	1	1	1	1
	1	1	1	1
3 3 1 1 1	3	1	1	
1 1 1 1 1 1 1 1	1	1	1	
1 1 1 1 1 1 1 1 1	3	1	1	
1 1 1 1 1 1 1 1 1	1	1	1	
3 3 5 1	3	1	1	
		1	1	
21	1	1		
			4	
20	4			
	2	2		
	1	1		
	2	2		
3	2	2		
7	1	1		
9	1	1		
11	1	2		
4 8	3	3		
13	10			
3 12	4	1		
6	9	1		
16	2			
13	3	3		
13	10			
11 1	4	1		
9	1	2		
7	2	1		
3	7			

47 DIFFICULTY ✪✪✪✪✩✩✩✩✩✩
Target time: 4 minutes

Each block is equal to the sum of the two numbers beneath it. Find all the missing numbers.

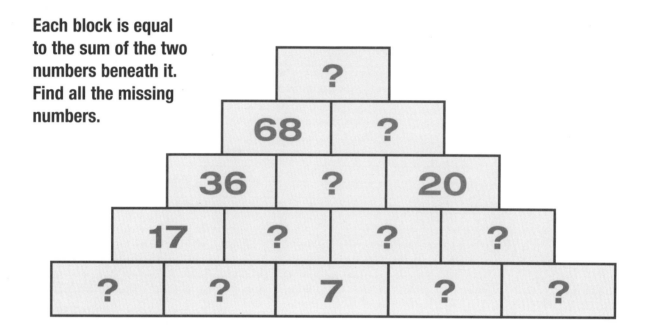

48 DIFFICULTY ✪✪✪✪✩✩✩✩✩✩
Target time: 3 minutes

Which number should replace the question mark in the following sequence?

10, 5, 12, 6, 16, 9, 22, ?

49 DIFFICULTY ✪✪✪✪✪✪✪✪☆☆

Target time: 6 minutes

Place the pieces from a standard set of twenty-eight dominoes into the following grid by matching their numbers with those in the rectangle. It's trickier than you think, so we've placed one in position to give you a start and supplied a checklist on the right that may help!

3	6	5	5	6	1	3
5	5	0	2	2	4	3
4	4	6	1	0	0	0
1	0	0	1	4	2	5
1	0	1	5	1	4	5
2	3	3	0	2	6	2
6	3	4	2	4	6	3
6	3	4	6	1	2	5

0/0	0/1	0/2	0/3	0/4	0/5	0/6
1/1	1/2	1/3	1/4	1/5	1/6	2/2
2/3	2/4	2/5	2/6	3/3	3/4	3/5
3/6	4/4	4/5	4/6	5/5	5/6	6/6

50 DIFFICULTY ✪✪✪✪✪✪✪✪✪✪

Target time: 6 minutes

			3	1			
3	5				4	5	
	1		2	4		2	
		3		1			
5					4		4
	2	3		5		1	
						2	

Can you divide this square into four identical shapes, each composed of sixteen smaller squares, and each containing five different numbers?

51 DIFFICULTY ✪✪✪✪✪✪✪✪✰✰
Target time: 5 minutes

Using three of the four different mathematical operators beneath each of the following three sums, can you achieve the correct totals, as given?

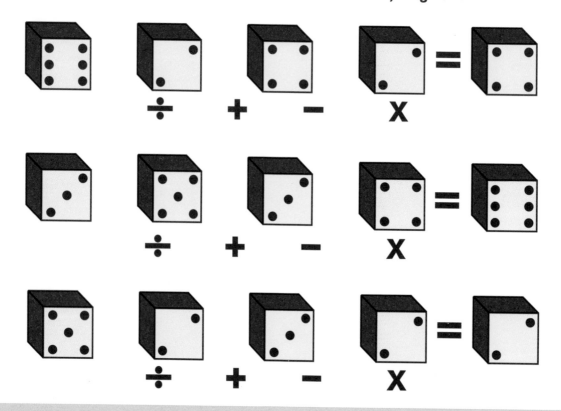

52 DIFFICULTY ✪✪✪✪✪✪✰✰✰✰
Target time: 3 minutes

Which is the odd number out?

$$2,743 \quad 2,917 \quad 9,461$$

$$9,172 \quad 6,813 \quad 4,819$$

$$3,724 \quad 1,836 \quad 9,418$$

53 DIFFICULTY ✪✪✪✪✪✪✪☆☆

Target time: 5 minutes

Fill in the missing number.

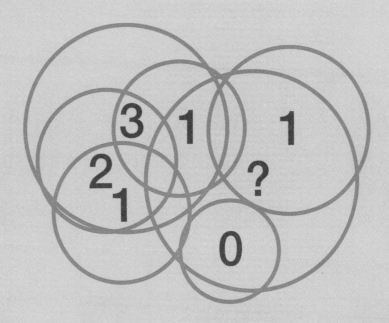

54 DIFFICULTY ✪✪✪✪☆☆☆☆☆☆

Target time: 3 minutes

Place a number in the middle box that divides into all the other numbers without leaving a remainder. The answer is greater than 1.

117   104

169   156

143   234

55 DIFFICULTY ✪✪✪✰✰✰✰✰✰✰
Target time: 6 minutes

Every row and column contains the same numbers and signs, but they are arranged in a different order each time. Find the correct order to arrive at the final totals shown.

7	x	4	−	2	+	5	=	31
							=	49
							=	13
							=	4
=		=		=		=		
8		10		23		16		

56 DIFFICULTY ✪✪✪✪✪✪☆☆☆☆

Target time: 6 minutes

Use one straight line to divide this circle into two sections, each with numbers adding up to the same total. Beware—all is not quite as it appears!

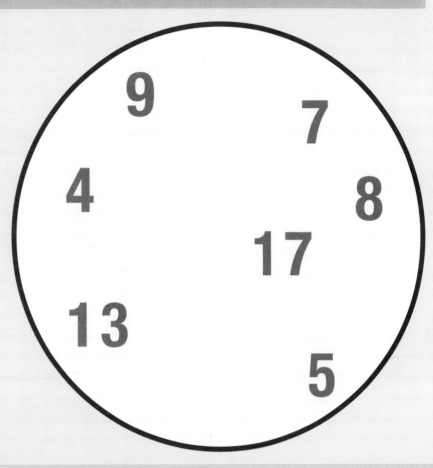

57 DIFFICULTY ✪✪✪☆☆☆☆☆☆☆

Target time: 2 minutes

What time should appear on the blank clock?

a   b   c   d   e

58 DIFFICULTY ✪✪✪✪✪✪✪✪✪✪

Target time: 3 minutes

Assess the cutlery below; given that scales a and b balance perfectly, how many knives are needed to balance scale c?

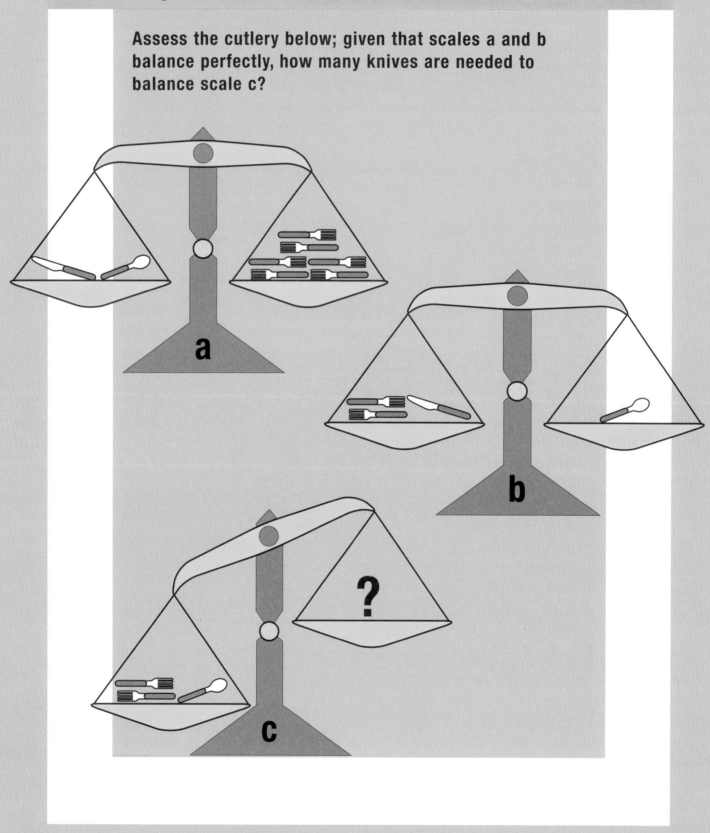

59 DIFFICULTY ✪✪✪✪✪✪✪✪✪

Target time: 8 minutes

Find the answers to the calculations in the grid, looking up, down, backward, forward, and diagonally.

1. 888 + 888
2. 1,111 x 7
3. 21,402 ÷ 2
4. 33 x 333
5. 7 x 7 x 7 x 7
6. 303,030 ÷ 3
7. 1,110 x 9
8. 1,000 – 506
9. 3,434 ÷ 2
10. 101 x 72
11. 88,888 ÷ 2 ÷ 2
12. (2,133 ÷ 3) + 3 + 3

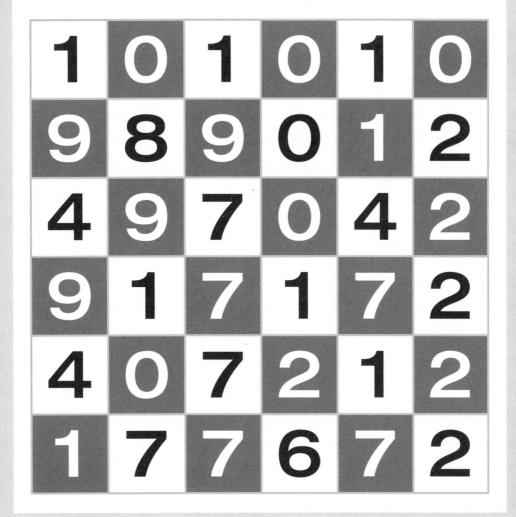

1	0	1	0	1	0
9	8	9	0	1	2
4	9	7	0	4	2
9	1	7	1	7	2
4	0	7	2	1	2
1	7	7	6	7	2

60 DIFFICULTY ✪✪✪✪✪✪✪✪✪✪
Target time: 8 minutes

Place the ace, king, queen, and jack of each suit so that:
* ★ no card value appears twice in any row, column, or main diagonal, and
* ★ no suit appears twice in any row, column, or main diagonal.

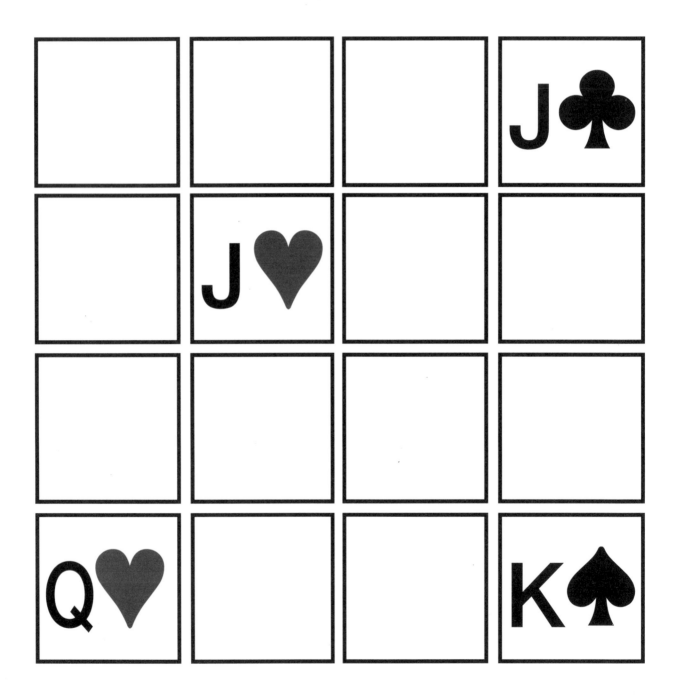

61 DIFFICULTY ✪✪✪✩✩✩✩✩✩✩
Target time: 3 minutes

Make a calculation totaling the figure below using some or all of the numbers above it and any of the four standard mathematical operators (+, −, x, and ÷).

1   6   7   8   9   10

= 476

62 DIFFICULTY ✪✪✪✪✩✩✩✩✩✩
Target time: 4 minutes

Replace the question marks with mathematical symbols to produce the correct answer. Only the four basic operators (+, −, x, and ÷) are permitted. Perform calculations in strict left to right order. Can you find two possible solutions?

7 ? 6 ? 5 ? 4

= 2

63 DIFFICULTY ✪✪✪✪✪✪✪✪☆☆

Target time: 10 minutes

This is a one-player solitaire game. Place two silver coins on spaces 1 and 2, and two pennies on spaces 9 and 10. The aim is to make the coins swap sides by sliding them along the lines.

However, there is a catch. At no point must a silver coin and a penny lie on the same line—for example, your opening move cannot be 2 to 4, because the silver coin at 4 and the penny at 9 would be on the same line. Also, only one coin per space is allowed.

How many moves are there in the shortest solution? One move counts as sliding one coin from one space along a straight line to another space, possibly moving through other spaces along the way, although if you wish to move the same coin along another line in a different direction, it counts as a second move.

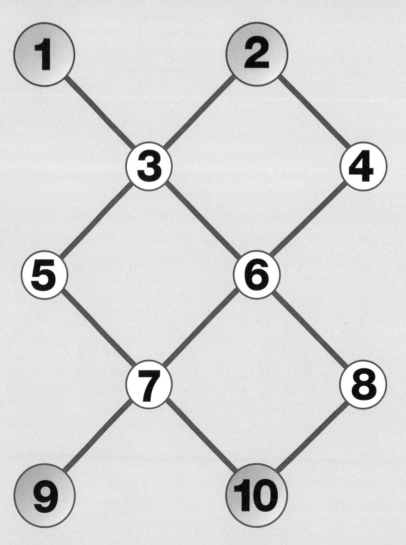

64 DIFFICULTY ✪✪✪✪✪✪✪✪☆☆

Target time: 5 minutes

Given that scales a and b balance perfectly, how many apples are needed to balance scale c?

65 DIFFICULTY ✪✪✪✪✪✪✪✪✪✪
Target time: 10 minutes

Can you fit these numbers into the grid? One number has already been inserted to help you get started.

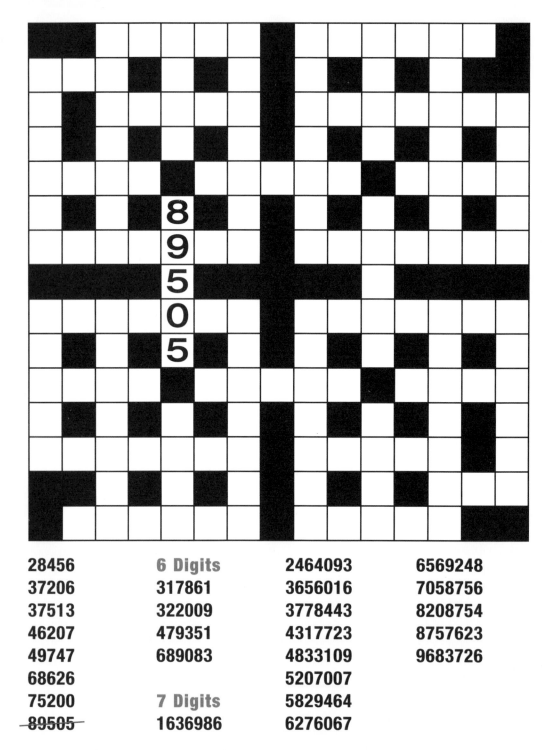

3 Digits
323
669

4 Digits
2056
3212
5430
6742
7733
8060
8179
9055

5 Digits
14355
21845

28456
37206
37513
46207
49747
68626
75200
~~89505~~

6 Digits
317861
322009
479351
689083

7 Digits
1636986

2464093
3656016
3778443
4317723
4833109
5207007
5829464
6276067

6569248
7058756
8208754
8757623
9683726

66 DIFFICULTY ✪✪✪✪✪✪✪✪✪✪

Target time: 4 minutes

The number 1,970,157 appears just once in this grid and occurs in a straight line, running either backward or forward in a horizontal, vertical, or diagonal direction. Can you locate it?

1	9	5	1	9	7	0	9	7	5	9	1
9	7	1	7	9	5	0	1	5	7	9	9
5	0	0	9	0	9	0	1	1	9	1	1
0	9	7	5	9	7	7	9	7	0	7	7
9	5	1	9	1	5	1	0	0	5	0	0
7	9	7	0	5	7	9	9	1	7	9	9
1	1	5	7	0	1	1	0	0	5	1	5
7	7	0	9	9	5	7	0	7	9	1	7
0	0	1	5	9	9	9	5	9	1	7	1
5	7	0	0	1	0	1	7	0	9	5	7
9	9	7	0	5	9	0	7	1	5	7	0
1	1	5	9	1	7	5	9	0	7	9	1

67 DIFFICULTY ✪✪✪✪✪✪✪✪☆✪

Target time: 6 minutes

Which number comes next?

$$2\tfrac{3}{4}, \quad 13\tfrac{3}{4}, \quad 5\tfrac{1}{4},$$

$$9\tfrac{1}{2}, \quad 7\tfrac{3}{4}, \quad 5\tfrac{1}{4}, \quad ?$$

68 DIFFICULTY ✪✪✪☆✪☆✪✪✪✪

Target time: 4 minutes

Each block is equal to the sum of the two numbers beneath it.
Find all the missing numbers.

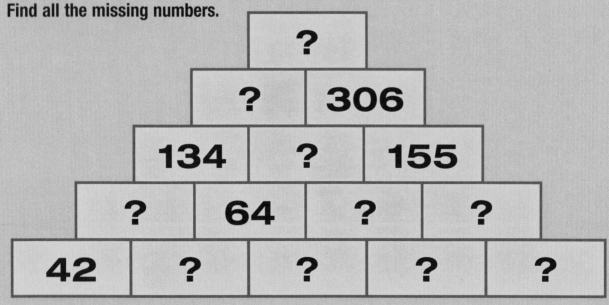

69 DIFFICULTY ✪✪✪✪✪✪✩✩✩✩
Target time: 3 minutes

Which is the odd number out?

3, 8, 15, 24, 29, 35, 48

70 DIFFICULTY ✪✪✪✪✪✪✪✩✩✩
Target time: 5 minutes

Adam and his sister Florence had a pair of standard dice and were playing a game where each needed to throw a double to start. On his very first turn, Adam threw a double six.

1. How likely was Florence to throw a double six on her next throw?

2. How likely was she to throw any double on her next throw?

3. What were the chances of Florence throwing, say, both a one and a six on her next throw?

4. How likely was she to throw her favorite number, four, on either of the die on her next throw?

71 DIFFICULTY ✪✪✪✪✪✪✪✪✪✪
Target time: 8 minutes

Place the ace, king, queen, and jack of each suit so that:
* no card value appears twice in any row, column, or main diagonal, and
* no suit appears twice in any row, column, or main diagonal.

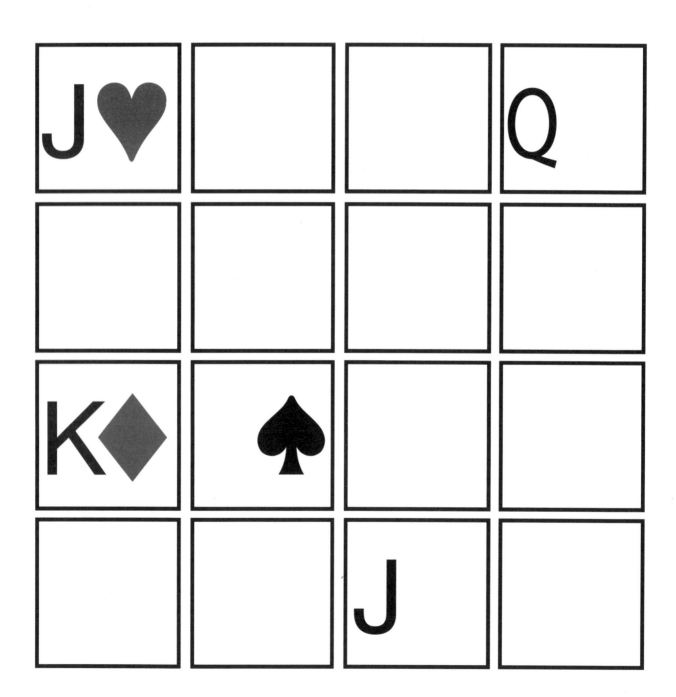

72 DIFFICULTY ★★★★★★★☆☆
Target time: 8 minutes

Make a calculation totaling the figure below using some or all of the numbers above it and any of the four standard mathematical operators (+, −, x, and ÷).

2   4   6   7   8   9

= *628*

73 DIFFICULTY ★★★★★★★★☆
Target time: 6 minutes

The cards on the right are valued as follows: an ace = 1, a jack = 11, a queen = 12, and a king = 13. All the other cards have the same value as their numbers.

Study this card arrangement carefully for one minute, then see if you can answer the questions on page 58 without checking back.

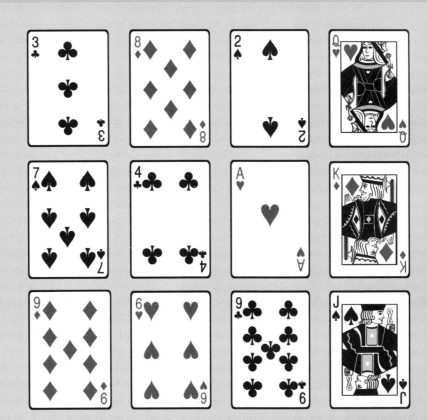

74 DIFFICULTY ✪✪✪✪✪✪✪☆☆
Target time: 6 minutes

Place a number in the middle box that divides into all the other numbers without leaving a remainder. The answer is greater than 1.

259   222

333   148

407   111

[73] DIFFICULTY ✪✪✪✪✪✪✪✪✪✪
Target time: 6 minutes

Can you answer these questions about the puzzle on page 57 without having to check back?

1. Which two numbers do not appear?

2. Which is the only pair of identical numbers to appear?

3. What is the highest total value of three cards in a column?

4. Two rows of four cards have the same total. What is this?

5. Which card is in the same column as (and directly below) a diamond, as well as being in the same column as (and directly above) a heart?

6. What is the total value of the four corner cards?

75 DIFFICULTY ✪✪✪✪✪✪✪✪☆☆

Target time: 10 minutes

Can you fit these numbers into the grid? One number
has already been inserted to help you get started.

3 Digits
371
863

4 Digits
1756
2186
4096
5559
6058
7206
8282
9976

5 Digits
11654
24663
~~32134~~
33848
42676

58520
66750
72055
82518
94194

6 Digits
642001
704118

835656
861703

7 Digits
1429538
1704156
2138713
2752146
3458232

3495012
4805632
5819673
6157413
6720466
7137525
8561716
8744934
9357045

Assess the symbols below. Given that scales a and b balance perfectly, how many spades are needed to balance scale c?

77 DIFFICULTY ✪✪✪✪✪✪✪✪☆☆

Target time: 5 minutes

Consider the celestial bodies below. Given that scales a and b balance perfectly, how many suns are needed to balance scale c?

78 DIFFICULTY ✪✪✪✪✪✪✪✪✪✪

Target time: 8 minutes

Find the answers to the following calculations
in the grid below, reading up, down, backward,
forward, and diagonally.

1. 10,000 – 5,454
2. 66 x 99
3. 4,224 x 2
4. 20,000 – 9,912
5. 52,000 ÷ 8
6. 5,555 – 4,321

7. 500 x 120
8. 1,604 x 5
9. 63,636 ÷ 3
10. (7 x 7) x (8 x 8)
11. 6,003 – 2,997
12. 101 x 10 x 9

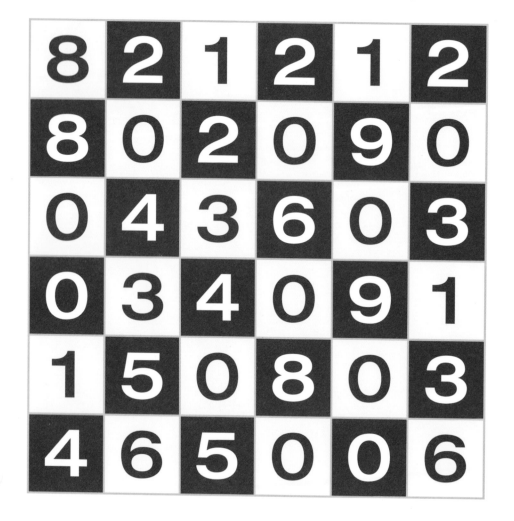

79 DIFFICULTY ✪✪✪✪✩✩✩✩✩✩
Target time: 3 minutes

Use two straight lines to divide this clock face into three parts, each containing numbers adding up to the same total.

80 DIFFICULTY ✪✪✪✪✪✪✩✩✩✩
Target time: 5 minutes

What number comes next in the sequence below?

-76, -27, -57, -46, -38, -65, ?

81 DIFFICULTY ✪✪✪✪✪✪✰✰✰✰
Target time: 6 minutes

Each block is equal to the sum of the two numbers beneath it.
Find all the missing numbers.

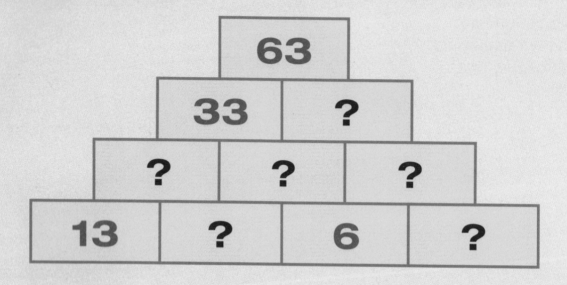

82 DIFFICULTY ✪✪✪✪✪✪✰✰✰✰
Target time: 3 minutes

Which number is the odd one out?

133, 171, 208, 247, 285

83 DIFFICULTY ✪✪✪✪✪✪✩✩✩
Target time: 7 minutes

Every row and column contains the same numbers and signs, but they are arranged in a different order each time. Find the correct order to arrive at the final totals shown.

20	+	5	−	11	x	6	=	84
							=	119
							=	125
							=	41
=		=		=		=		
75		95		69		65		

84 DIFFICULTY ✪✪✪✪✪✪✪✪✪✪
Target time: 6 minutes

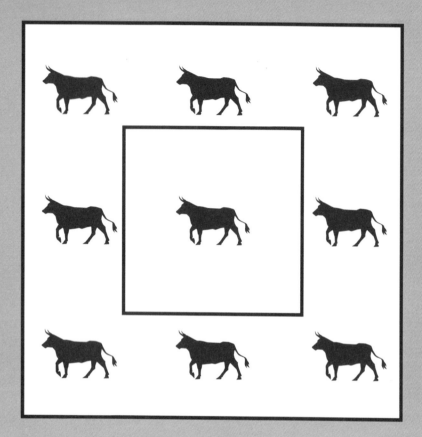

How many more square fences do you need to add so that each bull is separate from all the others?

85 DIFFICULTY ✪✪✪✪✪✪✪✪✪✪
Target time: 6 minutes

What number should replace the question mark in the following sequence?

365, 195, 380, 240, 395, 285, 410, ?

86 DIFFICULTY ✪✪✪✪✪✪✪✩✩✩

Target time: 20 minutes

Use skill (rather than luck) to solve this nonogram. (See page 18 for advice on how to complete a nonogram.)

Column clues (top):

1				2	1								2		1		5									10	10	
2	1		3	1	1								2	1	1		2	1						10	10	10	10		2	2	
5	5		2	1	1				5	5			7	2	5	1	3	1	7						3	3	3	1		1	1	10
4	2	2	2	2	2	2	2			1	2	2	1	3	1	3					2	2	2	1		10	3	3	1
5	1	3	3	3	1	2	3	3	5	5	2	2	2	3	2	2	2			2	2	2	1		10	3	3	1
6	12	12	1	1	1	12	12	1	1	2	8	2	2	2	2	2	2	2	3	2	2	2	1	10	2	1	1	11	10
10	10	10	10	10	10	10	10	10	10	3	12	2	2	2	12	2	2	2	12	2	2	2	12	3	11	1	2	3	4

Row clues (left):

- 6 10
- 5 12 10
- 4 8 1 10
- 3 1 4 1 1 10
- 2 1 8 2 10
- 1 12 3 10
- 4 10
- 12 5 10
- 12 2 2 10
- 2 2 2 1 1 10
- 2 2 2 1
- 2 2 2 1 2 3 2
- 12 2 3 2
- 12 13
- 11 2 3 2 1
- 2 2 2 3 2 2
- 2 2 1 1
- 2 2 13 1 1
- 9 13 1 1
- 1 1 1 1 1 2
- 10 1 1 1 1 4
- 10 1 1 1 1 4
- 10 13 2 1
- 10 13 1 1
- 10 1 1 1 1 1 1
- 10 1 1 1 1 1 1
- 10 1 1 1 1 2 1
- 10 13 1 2
- 10 13 3
- 10 4

87 DIFFICULTY ✪✪✪✪✪✩✩✩✩✩
Target time: 3 minutes

What time should it be on clock f?

88 DIFFICULTY ✪✪✪✪✩✩✩✩✩✩
Target time: 4 minutes

Can you find either of the two possible solutions using any of the four standard mathematical operators (+, −, x, ÷)?

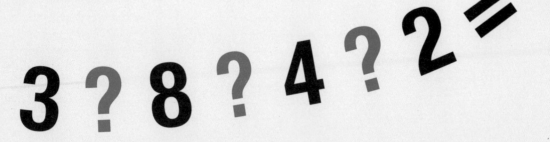

89 DIFFICULTY ✪✪✪✪✪✪✪✪☆☆
Target time: 8 minutes

Can you place the tiles in the grid so that:

* the odd numbers sit on the yellow spaces?
* the even numbers sit on the green spaces?
* each row, column, and main diagonal totals 34?

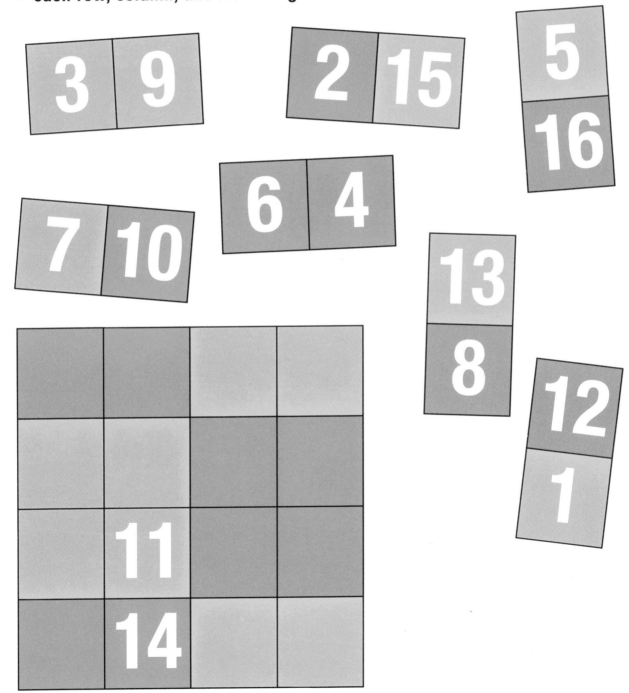

90 DIFFICULTY ✪✪✪✪✪✪✪✩✩✩

Target time: 10 minutes

Can you fit these numbers into the grid? One number has already been inserted to help you get started.

3 Digits
770
847

4 Digits
1805
2779
3586
4596
5358
6232
7519
8132

5 Digits
14385
23528
38923
46659
50658
61885
77576
82575
91513
92528

| 5 | 0 | 1 | 8 | 2 | 0 | 6 |

6 Digits
599560
784529
871625
934069

7 Digits
1353745
1379963
2455298
3129815

3199024
4505979
~~5018206~~
5757336
6208519

6714361
7070873
8171539
9033244
9726708

91 DIFFICULTY ✪✪✪✪✪✪✪☆☆

Target time: 10 minutes

The answers to the calculations below can be found in the grid—look up, down, backward, forward, and diagonally!

1. $(999 \div 3) \times 9^2$
2. $(2 + 2)^2 \times (3 + 3)^3$
3. 66×55
4. $(1{,}000{,}000 \div 50) \div 5$
5. $5{,}505.5 \times 2^4$
6. $(13{,}332 \times 2) \div 6$
7. $23 \times 24 \times 25$
8. $6{,}734 \times 3^2$
9. 101×11
10. 176×25
11. $(221 \div 13) + 1{,}717$
12. $163{,}216 \div 404$

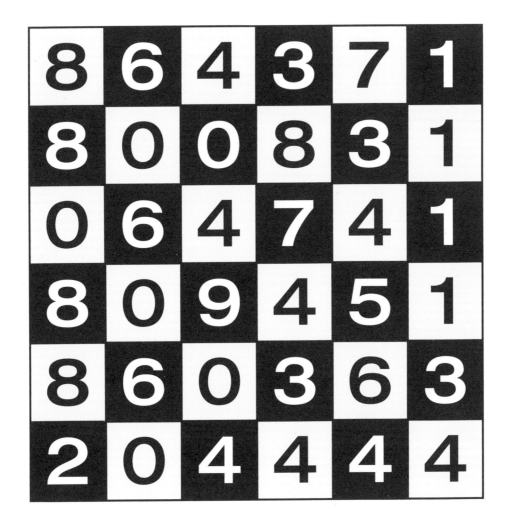

92 DIFFICULTY ✪✪✪✪✪✪✪✩✩

Target time: 6 minutes

How many squares on this miniature chess board can the knight visit (using his usual L-shaped move) without visiting a square twice?

93 DIFFICULTY ✪✪✪✪✩✩✩✩✩✩

Target time: 3 minutes

What is the sum total of the spots on the eleven hidden sides of these three dice?

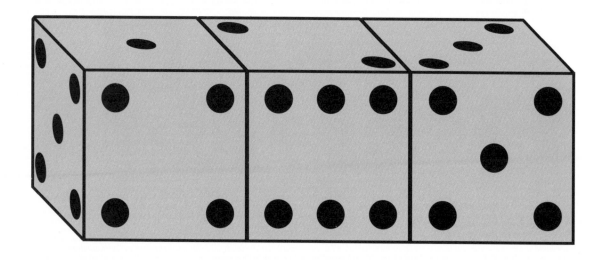

94 DIFFICULTY ✪✪✪✪✪✪✪☆☆
Target time: 6 minutes

Place a number in the middle box that divides into all the other numbers without leaving a remainder. The answer is greater than 1.

354		649
236		531
413		177

95 DIFFICULTY ✪✪✪✪✪✪☆☆☆☆
Target time: 3 minutes

Which number is the odd one out in this sequence?

7,246   **7,326**

7,270   **7,393**

7,297   **7,359**

96 DIFFICULTY ★★★★☆☆☆☆☆☆

Target time: 4 minutes

Replace the question marks with mathematical symbols to produce the correct answer. Only the four basic operators (+, −, x, and ÷) are permitted. Perform calculations in strict left to right order. Can you find all three possible solutions?

$$4 ? 3 ? 1 ? 2 = 9$$

97 DIFFICULTY ★★★★★☆☆☆☆☆

Target time: 4 minutes

Can you fit four different dominoes into the shape below, so that each horizontal and vertical line totals fourteen? We've placed two in their correct positions, although we haven't revealed how many dots (if any) should be on the second faces of these dominoes—you'll need to discover this, as well as the locations of the other dominoes, in order to arrive at the solution.

98 DIFFICULTY ✪✪✪✪✪✪✪✪✪✪
Target time: 7 minutes

The number 2,525,312 appears just once in this number-search grid and occurs in a straight line, running either backward or forward in a horizontal, vertical, or diagonal direction. Can you locate it?

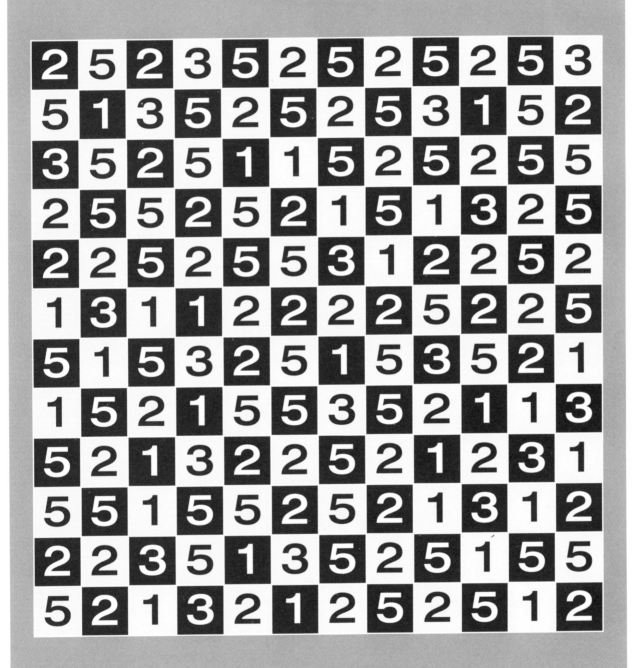

99 DIFFICULTY ✪✪✪✪✪✩✩✩✩

Target time: 6 minutes

Each block is equal to the sum of the two numbers beneath it. Find all the missing numbers.

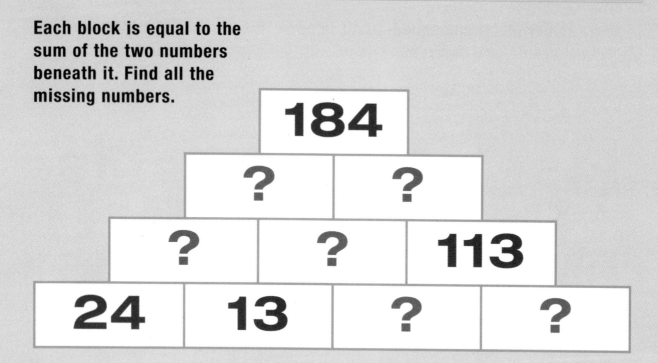

100 DIFFICULTY ✪✪✪✪✪✪✪✩✩✩

Target time: 7 minutes

Again, each block is equal to the sum of the two numbers beneath it. Find them all.

101 DIFFICULTY ✪✪✪✪✪✪✪✪✪✪

Target time: 10 minutes

Can you fit these numbers into the grid? One number has already been inserted to help you get started.

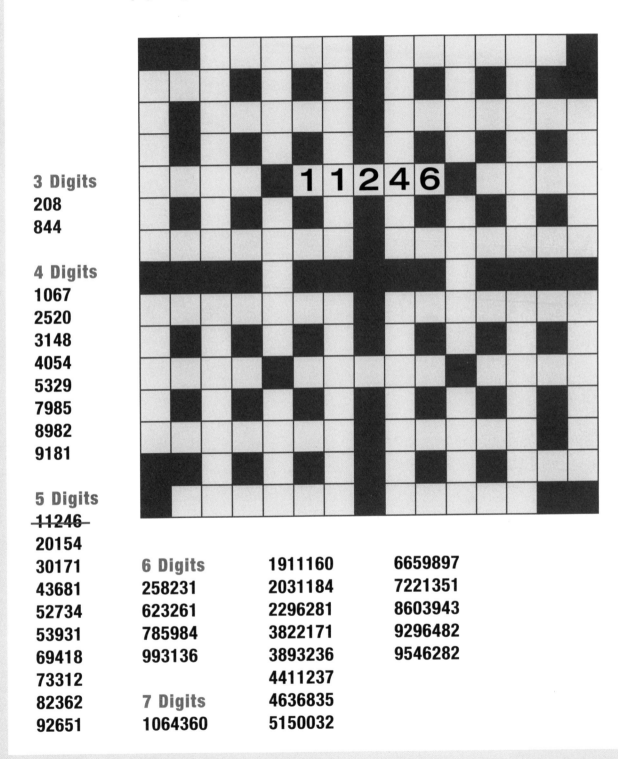

3 Digits
208
844

4 Digits
1067
2520
3148
4054
5329
7985
8982
9181

5 Digits
~~11246~~
20154
30171
43681
52734
53931
69418
73312
82362
92651

6 Digits
258231
623261
785984
993136

7 Digits
1064360

1911160
2031184
2296281
3822171
3893236
4411237
4636835
5150032

6659897
7221351
8603943
9296482
9546282

102 DIFFICULTY ✪✪✪✪✪✪✪✪✪✪

Target time: 6 minutes

Replace each star with a domino from the selection given below, so that the sum of every set of four connected by a black line is the same. One domino is already in position as a starter.

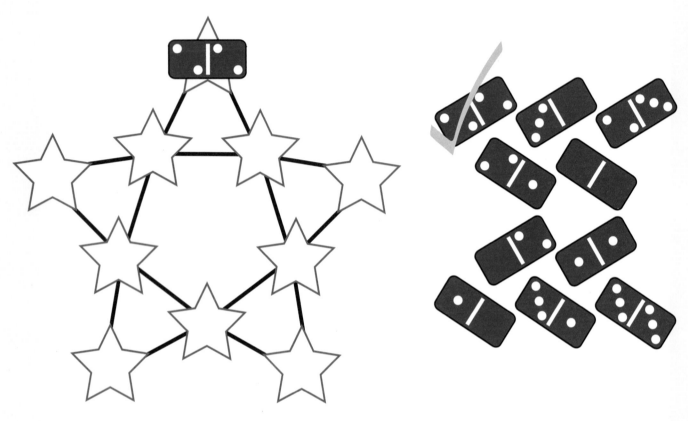

103 DIFFICULTY ✪✪✪✪✪✪✪✪✪✪

Target time: 5 minutes

What number should replace the question mark in the following sequence?

2,468, 8,652, 2,668, 8,672, ?

104 DIFFICULTY ✪✪✪✪✪✪✪✪✪

Target time: 10 minutes

The answers to the following calculations are embedded in the grid below—look up, down, backward, forward, and diagonally!

1. 24 x 365
2. 60 x 24 x 7
3. 60 x 60 x 24
4. 123,456 ÷ 3
5. (7 x 6 x 5) x (4 x 3 x 2)
6. (565 ÷ 5) x 13
7. 17.5% x 50,000
8. (888 ÷ 4) x 44
9. 10^2 x 9^2
10. 13,578 − 6,789
11. 198,198 ÷ 99

0	2	5	1	1	4
5	0	4	0	9	6
0	0	1	0	7	9
5	2	6	8	6	6
7	7	9	0	8	4
8	6	4	0	0	1

105 DIFFICULTY ✪✪✪✪✪✪✩✩✩✩
Target time: 6 minutes

What time should it be on clock f?

106 DIFFICULTY ✪✪✪✪✪✪✩✩✩✩
Target time: 6 minutes

Use three straight lines to divide this shape into four equally shaped sections, each containing three numbers adding up to the same total.

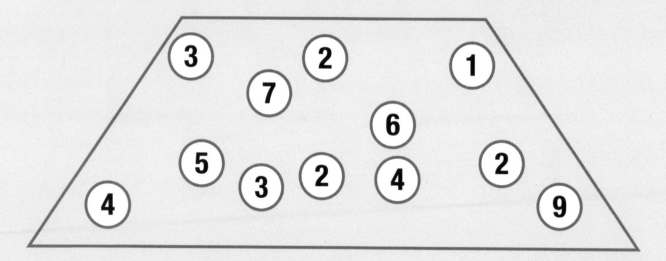

107 DIFFICULTY ✪✪✪✪✪✪✪✪✪✪

Target time: 6 minutes

2,166, 644, 1,255, 273, 819, 3,437, 5,128

Which is the odd number out?

108 DIFFICULTY ✪✪✪✪✪✪✪✪✪✪

Target time: 5 minutes

Juliette has lined up these three dice on her coffee table. She can see the same seven faces that you can see, and Angelica (her friend, sitting opposite) can see the top three faces of the dice, as well as a further four faces you and Juliette cannot see. None of you can see the bottom three faces of these dice. What is the total number of spots on all the faces of the dice that Angelica can see, given that this is a higher number than the total number of spots you can see?

109 DIFFICULTY ✪✪✪✪✪✪✪☆☆
Target time: 6 minutes

Place a number in the middle box that divides into all the other numbers without leaving a remainder. The answer is greater than 1.

141   517

376   611

564   423

110 DIFFICULTY ✪✪✪✪✪✪☆☆☆
Target time: 4 minutes

Moving east or south all the time, how many routes go from a to b that pass through one star at most?

111 DIFFICULTY ✪✪✪✪✪✰✰✰✰

Target time: 7 minutes

Every row and column contains the same numbers and signs, but they are arranged in a different order each time. Find the correct order to arrive at the final totals shown.

15	−	4	x	9	+	14	=	113
	■		■		■		■	
							=	225
	■		■		■		■	
							=	137
	■		■		■		■	
							=	35
=	■	=	■	=	■	=	■	
257	■	55	■	89	■	77	■	

112 DIFFICULTY ✪✪✪✪✪✪✰✰✰✰
Target time: 6 minutes

Each block is equal to the sum of the two numbers beneath. Find all the missing numbers (clue: Some contain fractions).

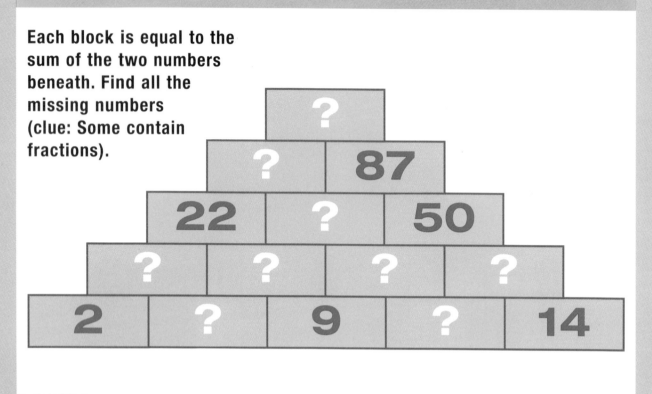

113 DIFFICULTY ✪✪✪✪✪✪✪✪✰✰
Target time: 6 minutes

What time should it be on clock e?

114 DIFFICULTY ✪✪✪✪✪✪✪☆☆
Target time: 8 minutes

Can you place the tiles in the grid so that:
* there is one square of every color in every row and column, and
* every row, column, and main diagonal totals 34?

115 DIFFICULTY ✪✪✪✪✪✩✩✩✩
Target time: 5 minutes

Can you find both of the possible solutions using any of the four standard mathematical operators (+, −, x, ÷)?

5 ? 19 ? 6

? 1 = 4

116 DIFFICULTY ✪✪✪✪✪✪✪✪✩
Target time: 6 minutes

Don't be alarmed! Study these clock radios carefully for ninty seconds, noting the station to which they are tuned, the actual time, and the time the alarm is due to go off, then see if you can answer the questions on page 88 without checking back.

Music 197
6:35 P.M.
🔔 6:35 A.M.

News 350
11:15 P.M.
🔔 5:55 A.M.

Sports 1532
12:25 A.M.
🔔 7:15 A.M.

Talk 820
10:40 P.M.
🔔 8:20 A.M.

117 DIFFICULTY ✪✪✪✪✪✪✪✪✪✪

Target time: 10 minutes

Can you fit these numbers into the grid? One number has already been inserted to help you get started.

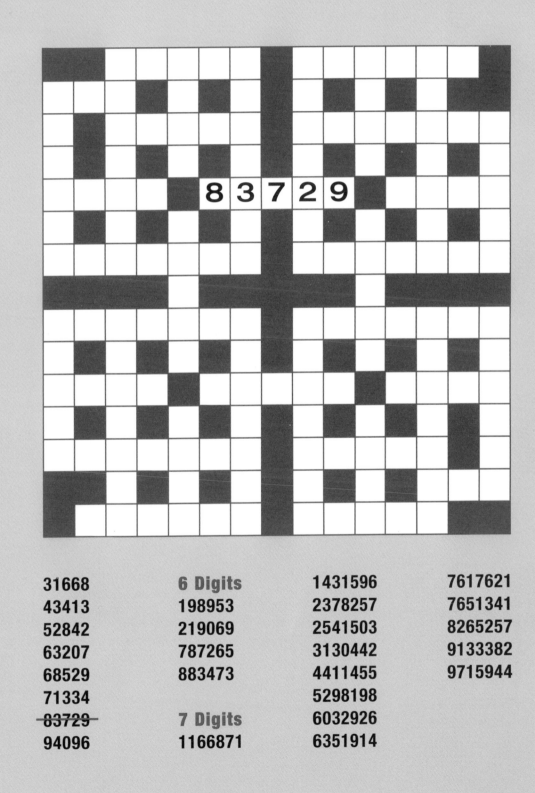

3 Digits
513
885

4 Digits
2812
3916
4854
5194
6902
7044
8638
9658

5 Digits
10681
22799

31668
43413
52842
63207
68529
71334
83729
94096

6 Digits
198953
219069
787265
883473

7 Digits
1166871

1431596
2378257
2541503
3130442
4411455
5298198
6032926
6351914

7617621
7651341
8265257
9133382
9715944

118 DIFFICULTY ✪✪✪✪✪✪✪✪✪✪

Target time: 5 minutes

Make a calculation totaling the figure on the right using some or all of the numbers below with any of the four standard mathematical operators (+, −, x, and ÷).

$$4 \quad 4 \quad 5 \quad 5 \quad 7 \quad 7 = 900$$

[116] DIFFICULTY ✪✪✪✪✪✪✪✪✪✪

Target time: 6 minutes

Can you answer these questions about the puzzle on page 86 without checking back?

1. The alarm on which color of clock radio is scheduled to go off at the latest time?

2. What station is tuned in on the clock radio with an alarm scheduled to go off exactly twelve hours later than its current time?

3. What is the current time on the station tuned to News 350?

4. What station is the sports channel?

5. Assuming each of the owners of the four pictured clock radios will fall asleep at exactly their clock's current time and will wake as soon as their alarm sounds, what station will the person who will have the least sleep be listening to when their alarm goes off?

6. What color is the clock radio that is tuned in to a channel that has the same number as the time of its alarm?

119 DIFFICULTY ✪✪✪✪✪✪✪✪✪

Target time: 5 minutes

Given that scales a and b balance perfectly, how many circles are needed to balance scale c?

120 DIFFICULTY ✪✪✪✪✪✪☆☆☆

Target time: 5 minutes

Which is the odd one out?

4,396   **4,250**   7,586

9,237   **4,805**   *9,782*

121 DIFFICULTY ✪✪✪✪✪✪✪☆☆

Target time: 10 minutes

The square below contains exactly one of each of the thirty-six faces from six standard dice. In each horizontal row of six smaller squares and each vertical column of six smaller squares, there are faces with different numbers of spots. There is no face with five spots in either of the two long diagonal lines of six smaller squares. The total number of spots in the diagonal line from top left to bottom right is seventeen, and that in the diagonal line from top right to bottom left is twenty-three. We've placed a few to give you a start, but can you place the rest?

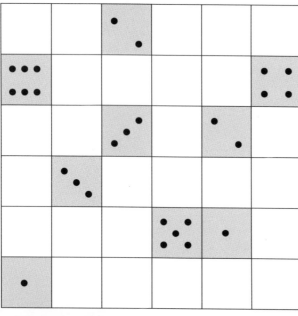

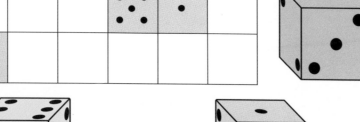

122 DIFFICULTY ✪✪✪✪✪✪✪✪✪✪

Target time: 10 minutes

The answers to the following calculations can be found in the grid—look up, down, backward, forward, and diagonally!

1. 22 x 33 x 44
2. (123 + 123) x 123
3. (989 − 323) x 6
4. (2 + 3) x (4 + 5) x (6 + 7) x (8 + 9)
5. $(9^2) \times (5^2)$
6. 76,544 + 123,456
7. 30,800 ÷ 7
8. 5.5 x 666
9. (111 x 3 x 3) + 2
10. 12,250 ÷ 35
11. $10^3 + 10$
12. 9,494 ÷ 2

2	0	0	0	0	0
0	0	8	5	0	5	4
2	5	3	1	4	7
5	2	0	9	9	4
1	0	1	0	9	7
1	3	6	6	3	6

123 DIFFICULTY ✪✪✪✪✪✪✪☆☆

Target time: 6 minutes

What is the smallest number of coins that need to be moved so that the coins inside one box total exactly twice the value of those in the other? Think laterally for this one!

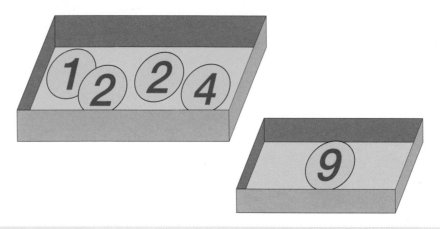

124 DIFFICULTY ✪✪✪✪✪✪☆☆☆

Target time: 5 minutes

Which number comes next?

1,447, 1,491, 1,540, 1,594, 1,653, ?

125 DIFFICULTY ✪✪✪✪✪✪✪✩✩✩
Target time: 4 minutes

What time should it be on clock e?

126 DIFFICULTY ✪✪✪✪✪✪✪✪✪✪
Target time: 8 minutes

Replace the question marks with mathematical symbols to produce the correct answer. Only the four basic operators (+, −, x, and ÷) are permitted. Perform calculations in strict left to right order. Can you find two possible solutions?

$$5 \; ? \; \tfrac{1}{2} \; ? \; \tfrac{1}{4}$$

$$? \; 6 = 8 \tfrac{1}{4}$$

127 DIFFICULTY ✩✩✩✩✩✩✩✩✩

Target time: 8 minutes

Can you place the tiles in the grid so that:

* the colors form a checkerboard pattern, and
* each row, column, and main diagonal totals the same number?

Note: Look at the tiles from all angles!

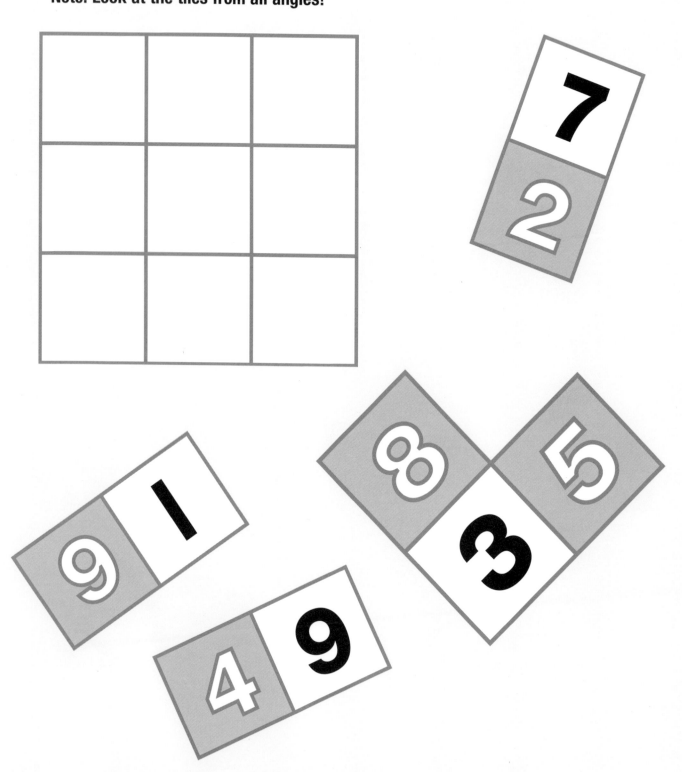

128 DIFFICULTY ✪✪✪✪✪✪✪✪✪✪
Target time: 8 minutes

Each block is equal to the sum of the two numbers
beneath it. Find all the missing numbers.

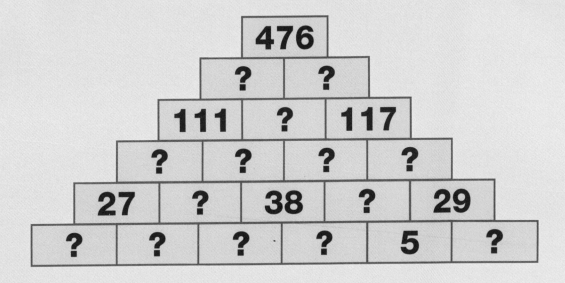

129 DIFFICULTY ✪✪✪✪✪✪✪✪✪✪
Target time: 5 minutes

Which number comes next?

34, 77, 154, 605, 1,111, ?

130 DIFFICULTY ✪✪✪✪✪✪✩✩✩✩
Target time: 5 minutes

Which number should take the place of the question mark?

18  6  2  ?

131 DIFFICULTY ✪✪✪✪✪✪✪✪✩✩
Target time: 6 minutes

Using a standard set of dominoes (as pictured here), start with the double blank and form a continuous snake by joining all but one of the dominoes end to end until you reach the double six. Dominoes must be joined according to the normal rules of the game, i.e., the adjacent sides of touching dominoes must always be the same. This can be achieved in many ways, but only if one domino is discarded. So which one is the domi-"no-no"?

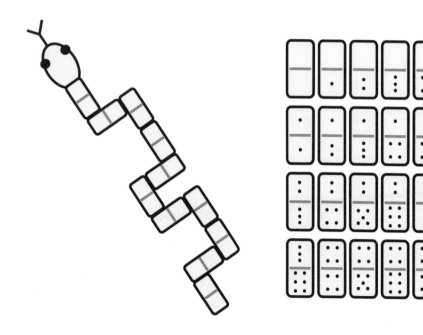

132 DIFFICULTY ✪✪✪✪✪✪✪✪☆☆
Target time: 5 minutes

Place a number in the middle box that divides into all the other numbers without leaving a remainder. The answer is greater than 1.

882		441
504		567
693		315

133 DIFFICULTY ✪✪✪✪✪✪✪✪✪✪
Target time: 10 minutes

Without lifting pencil from paper, draw straight lines to divide this heart into six parts, each containing four different numbers.

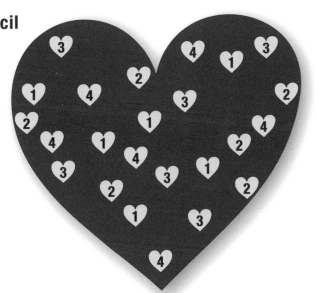

134 DIFFICULTY ✪✪✪✪✪✪✪✪✪✩

Target time: 6 minutes

What number should replace the question mark in the following sequence?

23, 28, 43, 65, 98, ?

135 DIFFICULTY ✪✪✪✪✪✪✩✩✩✩

Target time: 4 minutes

Where should the minute hand point on clock e?

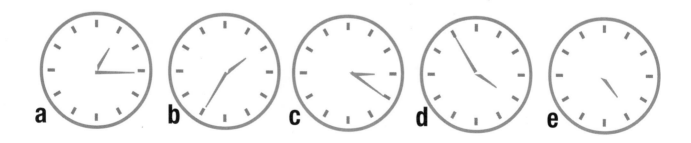

a   b   c   d   e

136 DIFFICULTY ✪✪✪✪✪✪✪✪✪✪
Target time: 8 minutes

Each block is equal to the sum of the two numbers beneath it.
Find all the missing numbers.

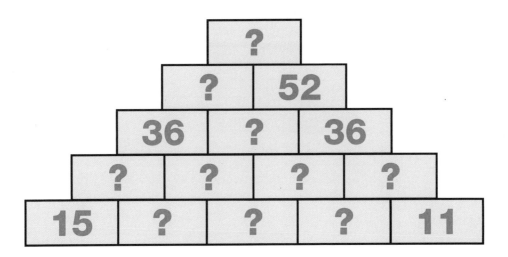

137 DIFFICULTY ✪✪✪✪✪✪✪☆☆☆
Target time: 3 minutes

Which number is the odd one out?

15, 24, 35, 48, 64, 80

138 DIFFICULTY ✪✪✪✪✪✪✪✪✪✪

Target time: 20 minutes

A right royal nonogram for all you cardsharks. (See page 18 for advice on how to complete a nonogram.)

															2	1	2	1											
				1											1	1	1	1	2	1				1					
				2		2		1	2				2	1	1	2	2	5	1	1	2		2	2					
4				1	2	1		1	12	1	3		15	1	2	1	1	2	1	2	1		2	5	1	1	6		
1				4	1	2	17	2	2	1	14	1	1	2	1	3	1	2	1	1	2		1	5	1	4	1		
1		10		1	1	2	2	2	3	2	2	1	2	1	1	1	1	1	1	3	3	16	1	4	2	1	1	5	
1		1	7	1	2	2	2	2	2	2	2	1	2	2	4	6	1	2	3	5	3	3	5	1	4	2	1	3	8
2	13	1	6	1	8	2	3	1	1	1	2	3	1	2	3	1	7	1	7	1	1	4	7	1	2	1	1	3	4

								2	1
		2	1	1	1	1	1	1	2
							2	1	13
								5	1
								1	11
								7	2
				1	1	1	1	1	1
				1	1	1	5	4	1
				1	1	1	2	3	4
			1	1	1	1	1	1	1
			1	1	1	1	1	1	1
			1	1	1	1	1	1	1
		1	1	1	1	1	3	1	1
		4	1	1	1	2	1	1	1
		2	1	1	1	1	3	2	2
	2	1	1	1	1	1	1	1	1
	8	1	1	1	2	1	1	2	2
		4	2	1	2	1	1	1	8
		5	2	1	1	1	4	2	4
	6	2	1	1	1	1	1	2	4
			7	2	2	1	2	3	5
	3	1	3	2	1	1	1	4	1
			3	1	2	2	2	3	6
					7	2	10	3	2
						3	17	2	4
	2	1	1	2	1	3	2	1	1
1	1	2	1	1	2	1	3	1	3
		8	1	1	1	3	1	4	2
	2	1	2	1	1	1	1	2	4
		1	2	1	2	1	6	3	1

139 DIFFICULTY ✪✪✪✪✪✪☆☆☆☆

Target time: 5 minutes

Make a calculation totaling the figure below, using some or all of the numbers above it with any of the four standard mathematical operators (+, –, x, and ÷).

4 7 9 10 25 75

= 924

140 DIFFICULTY ✪✪✪✪☆☆☆☆☆☆

Target time: 4 minutes

These dominoes follow a certain sequence, so can you tell what should be in the empty space?

141 DIFFICULTY ✪✪✪✪✪✪✪✪✪✪
Target time: 6 minutes

Which is the odd number out?

5,431   *5,437*

5,449   **5,464**

5,471   5,477

142 DIFFICULTY ✪✪✪✪✪✪✪✪✪✪
Target time: 7 minutes

What number should replace the question mark in the following sequence?

75,634, 48,192, ?, 7,320, 1,460

143 DIFFICULTY ✪✪✪✪✪✪✪✪✪
Target time: 10 minutes

The answers to the calculations below can be found in the grid—look up, down, backward, forward, and diagonally!

1. (2 x 3 x 4) x (5 x 6 x 7)
2. 123 x 321
3. 2 x 22 x 222
4. 5,656 + 7,878
5. 220^2
6. 10,000 − 6,666 − 666 − 66 − 6
7. (99 − 2) x (99 + 2)
8. 71,104 ÷ 8
9. (26,400 ÷ 2) ÷ 3
10. (747 x 5) x 2
11. 14^4

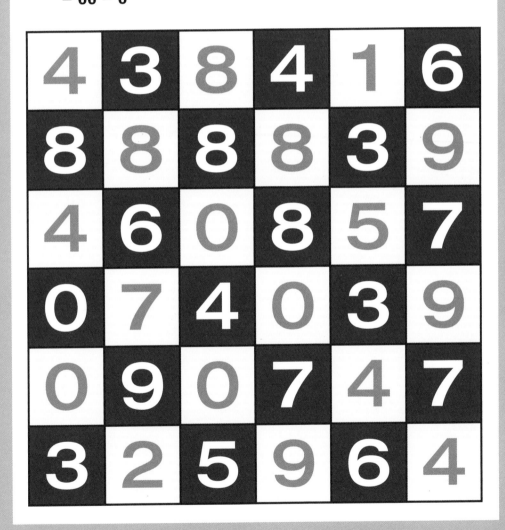

4	3	8	4	1	6
8	8	8	8	3	9
4	6	0	8	5	7
0	7	4	0	3	9
0	9	0	7	4	7
3	2	5	9	6	4

144 DIFFICULTY ✪✪✪✪✪✪✪✪✪✩✩
Target time: 7 minutes

Replace the question marks with mathematical symbols to produce the correct answer. Only the four basic operators (+, −, x, and ÷) are permitted. Perform calculations in strict left to right order. Can you find all three possible solutions?

24 ? 6 ? 9 ? 2

=18

145 DIFFICULTY ✪✪✪✪✪✪✪✪✪✪
Target time: 6 minutes

When these four tiles are arranged correctly, the pattern shown is a continuous loop. What is the least number of 90-degree revolutions needed to achieve this. Some lateral thinking may be necessary!

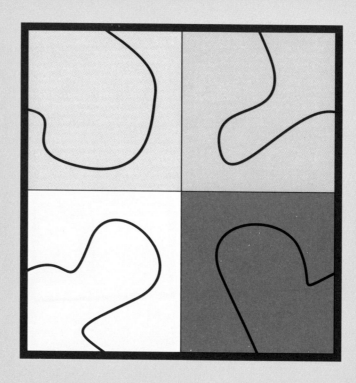

146 DIFFICULTY ✪✪✪✪✪✪✪✪✪✪✪

Target time: 8 minutes

Can you place the tiles in the grid so that:

* each row and column contains three squares of each color, and
* each row and column contains exactly one of each number?

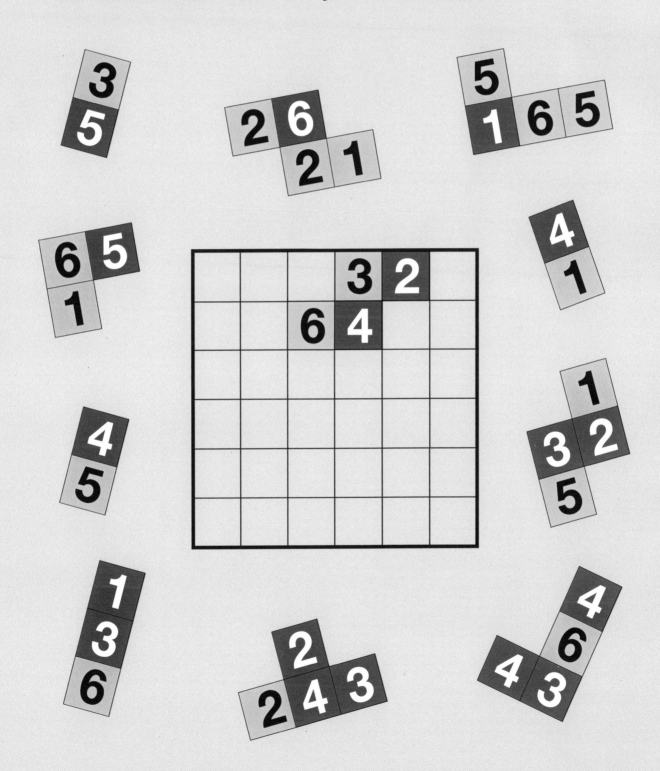

ANSWERS

1

1	2	3	4
4	1	2	3
2	3	4	1
3	4	1	2

2

```
 1 0 7 4 3   7 8 7 4 1 8
8 1 1   1   5   3   2   7
7   9 4 7 4 2   4 6 9 8 3 8 2
4   3   3   9   1   0   6   7
6 5 7 8   3 4 7 4 9   2 4 6 6
4   8   7   9   4   8   5   2
4 6 8 7 3 3 3   2 4 0 2 3 2 6
        8           7
6 4 8 0 1 8 3   5 3 5 9 6 8 1
1   9   1   2   6   3   7   1
6 3 1 6   1 4 9 2 0   1 3 0 5
2   4   3   1   1   5   4   8
3 1 9 3 2 1 0   5 1 3 4 9   0
    1   6   9   9   9   6 9 0
  4 3 2 8 3 6   9 2 6 0 7
```

3

(25 x 5 x 4) + (9 x 3) = 527
There are ten other
possible solutions.

4

1. **19**
2. **1 + 2 + 3 = 6**
3. **7**
4. **Green**
5. **2 (1 and 3)**
6. **9**
7. **4**
8. **2**

5

b; the other three have
the same angle between
the hands.

6

Follow the route marked
by the red squares:
(3 x 5 + 3 ÷ 6 + 2 − 1 = 4)

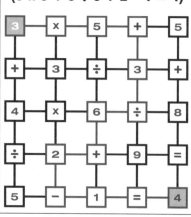

7

Three; each apple weighs as much as two oranges, and each banana weighs as much as four oranges. Thus three apples are needed to balance scale c.

8

1. 6,561
2. 2,000
3. 1,232
4. 10,100
5. 352
6. 6,170
7. 2,904
8. 1,000
9. 7,654
10. 1,782
11. 520
12. 30,330
13. 2,260

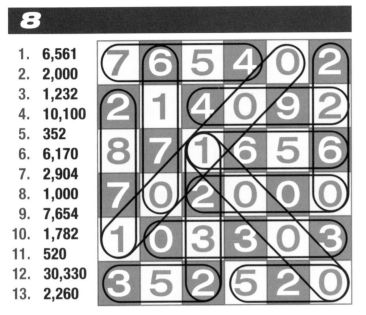

9

3	+	2	x	6	–	5	=	25
x		x		–		–		
6	–	3	x	5	+	2	=	17
+		+		+		x		
5	+	6	–	2	x	3	=	27
–		–		x		+		
2	+	5	–	3	x	6	=	24
=		=		=		=		
21		7		9		15		

10

Remove one coin from the bottom row to leave five coins remaining. The crux of the problem is the single coin in the top row, and uses logic of odd and even numbers. If your opponent takes it at any stage, make sure your next move leaves the two larger rows equal in coins. Until that happens, ensure that the two larger rows are one coin different (e.g., 2 and 3).

11

5	4	3	7	9	8	7	3	5	4	9	5
9	8	3	5	9	3	7	5	3	4	8	4
3	4	7	5	4	3	5	9	5	3	7	7
4	5	4	9	4	5	8	4	7	3	9	3
5	4	3	7	9	3	3	8	5	9	8	8
9	3	4	8	5	7	9	9	4	9	9	9
4	7	9	4	9	8	9	7	7	3	4	5
8	5	9	5	4	3	5	8	9	8	8	3
7	9	5	3	5	9	8	7	3	4	5	9
5	1	4	7	4	8	7	5	9	7	5	3
8	5	3	5	3	3	4	9	5	8	4	4
9	8	7	3	5	4	5	4	3	9	7	8

12

		7	6	1	5	4		9	4	2	8	2	9	
8	7	7		8		9		4		5		5		
2		7	3	2	1	4		6	4	9	8	8	7	7
8		6		1		8		1		4		6		1
7	2	6	3		2	0	9	0	1		2	6	8	0
3		7		3		8		3		5		4		4
6	0	2	9	2	5	7		1	4	1	9	6	9	4
				8						2				
7	4	7	2	5	1	7		6	8	1	7	5	1	1
5		9		0		6		0		5		6		1
1	5	7	2		2	4	4	4	3		7	4	2	5
5		2		2		7		8		9		5		6
9	8	7	7	7	6	8		9	7	4	9	2		9
		3		5		8		3		8		3	1	5
		7	3	9	7	1	5		3	0	4	0	5	

13

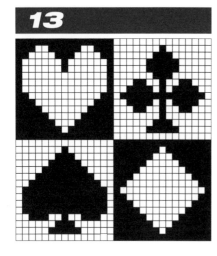

14

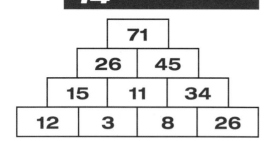

15

b is at (9, 6) and d is at (5, 0). The secret is to work out that the average of a and c's coordinates give the center of the square as (7, 3).

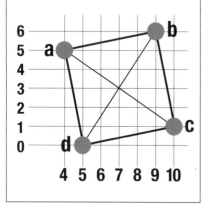

16

486; all the others have their digits in ascending order.

17

((6 ÷ 2) x 3) + 7 = 16;   (6 x 2) − 3 + 7 = 16

18

5	4	3	1
2	1	4	3
4	3	1	5
3	2	5	4

19

21

20

Gary won $4. The total payback is three times the difference of the number of spots on the two dice. Thus Gary got back $9: (5 − 2) x 3 = 9, winning $4.

21

Ten; from b we can infer that three moons equals one star; from a we can thus infer that seven moons equals five suns. If we then convert the left-hand side of c into moons we get fourteen moons (because each star is worth three moons). As we know that seven moons equals five suns, we can deduce that twice that will need ten suns to balance scale c.

22

91.25; deduct 1.25, then 2.5 alternately.

23

80; write the points as digits, then add them up in rows:

a. 13 + 21 = 34
b. 40 + 11 = 51
c. 26 + 45 = 71
so d. 45 + 35 = 80

24

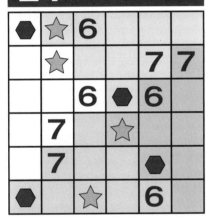

25

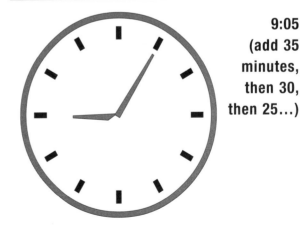

26

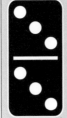

a; the dots in the upper part of each domino increase in number by one every time, while those in the lower part decrease by one every time, thus the total number of dots on each domino remains the same every time.

27   ## 28

17

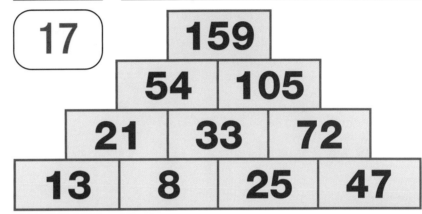

29

4,569; in all the others the third digit is the sum of the first two digits, and the fourth digit is the sum of the second and third digits.

30

9:05 (add 35 minutes, then 30, then 25...)

31

12 − 4 + 7 − 8 = 7
((12 − 4) x 7) ÷ 8 = 7

32

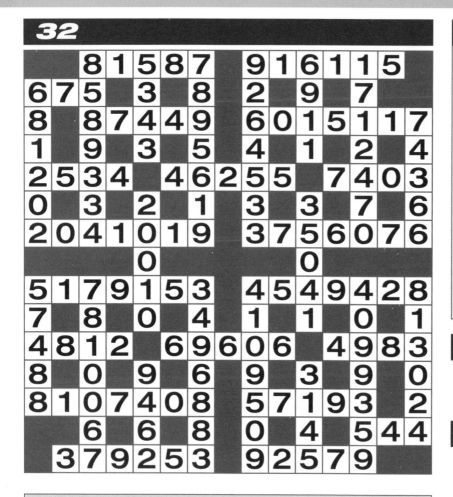

33

Fourteen; one spade weighs as much as four clubs, and one heart weighs as much as six clubs. Thus fourteen clubs are needed to balance scale c.

34

42; all of the others are prime numbers.

35

Gary won $8. The total payback is the number of points on the first die multiplied by the number of points on the second. Thus Gary got back $20 (5 x 4 = 20), winning $8.

36

1.	41,976
2.	3,375
3.	1,616
4.	2,200
5.	23,456
6.	303
7.	1,551
8.	5,555
9.	444
10.	3,125
11.	765
12.	656

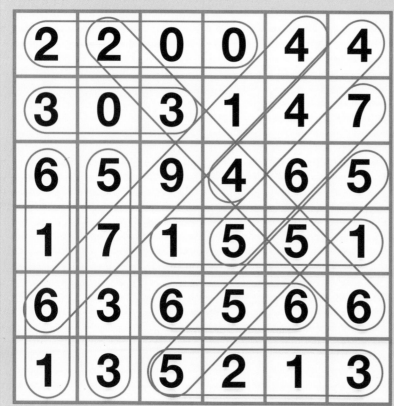

37

1. 2; the triangle (7) and pentagon (23)
2. 16 + 7 = 23
3. 4 x 16 = 64
4. Triangle (7) and pentagon (23)
5. Pink (16), blue (4), and lilac (46)
6. 35; 7 + 4 = 11, 46 − 11 = 35

38

The Pythagorean Theorem. Consider Fig. 1. The length of this square's sides is the same as the hypotenuse (longest side) of any of the triangles. In Fig. 2, we have rearranged the same shapes into a different configuration, so the areas must be equal. There are two squares (separated by the dotted line). The left-hand square has sides equivalent to the middle-length side of the triangle, while the sides of the right-hand square are equal to the triangle's shortest side. In other words, the square of the hypotenuse is equal to the sum of the squares of the other two sides, which is the Pythagorean Theorem.

39

(((7 x 4) + 4) x 10) − 9 = 311. There are thirteen other possible solutions.

40

1	8	0	4	8	7	0	9	1	8	0	4
4	7	8	0	9	8	1	9	9	8	1	0
4	1	0	0	7	9	8	9	1	7	4	0
7	8	9	0	1	4	7	0	9	1	9	8
4	9	0	4	7	8	4	8	1	0	7	7
8	9	8	7	0	9	0	8	9	0	0	9
9	0	7	9	4	8	9	1	4	9	0	4
8	8	4	9	8	1	9	4	9	7	8	9
1	0	7	8	4	9	0	1	8	9	4	9
9	7	9	1	4	0	1	8	0	9	8	0
4	9	8	0	8	4	0	8	1	4	7	8
8	7	1	1	4	1	9	8	7	9	1	1

41

			3	3			
		1					
		1		2		1	1
			4	4	2		
2	2						3
	4						3
	4						

42

43

11

44

846; it should be 847 since each number is reversed then added on to the previous number.

45

Follow the route marked in green.

66	14	18	65	26	55	19
77	50	21	16	49	24	63
75	33	37	78	40	54	10
96	98	96	25	18	15	36
31	20	36	49	54	50	56
98	48	11	23	91	72	56
20	28	45	78	91	15	72
12	23	54	77	85	95	21
16	25	24	66	14	91	40

46

49

50

			3	1		
3 5					4 5	
	1		2	4		2
			3		1	
5					4		4
	2 3			5		1
						2

47

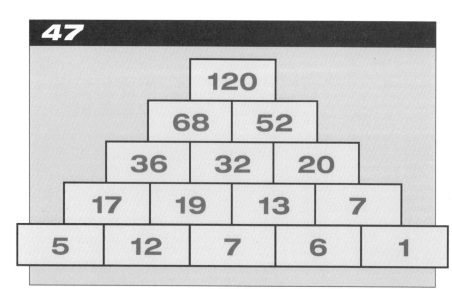

48

14; there are two sequences running alternately.
Starting with 10, add 2, 4, 6, etc.
Starting with 5, add 1, 3, 5, etc.
So 9 + 5 = 14.

51

((6 x 2) − 4) ÷ 2 = 4
((3 + 5) x 3) ÷ 4 = 6
(5 + 2 − 3) ÷ 2 = 2

52

9,461; the rest can be
paired off into anagrams
of one another:
2,743–3,724;
9,172–2,917;
6,813–1,836;
4,819–9,418.

53

3; because the big circle centered around that number encompasses three of the other numbers (1, 1, and 0). The other big circle has a 3 at the center; it, too, encompasses three numbers (1, 1, and 2).

54

13

55

7	x	4	–	2	+	5	=	31
–		x		+		+		
5	–	2	+	4	x	7	=	49
x		+		x		–		
2	x	7	–	5	+	4	=	13
+		–		–		x		
4	+	5	–	7	x	2	=	4
=		=		=		=		
8		10		23		16		

56

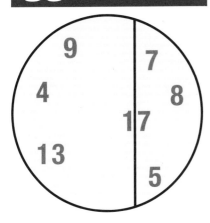

9 7

4 8

13 17

5

57

3:55 (add 1 hour and 25 minutes each time).

58

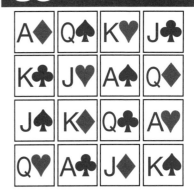

Three; one knife weighs as much as two forks, and two knives weigh as much as one spoon. Thus three knives are needed to balance scale c.

59

1. 1,776
2. 7,777
3. 10,701
4. 10,989
5. 2,401
6. 101,010
7. 9,990
8. 494
9. 1,717
10. 7,272
11. 22,222
12. 717

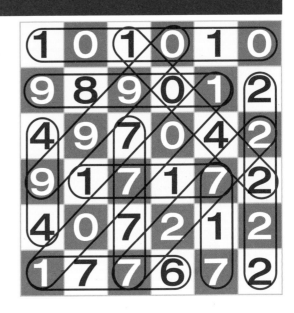

60

A♦	Q♠	K♥	J♣
K♣	J♥	A♠	Q♦
J♠	K♦	Q♣	A♥
Q♥	A♣	J♦	K♠

61

$((10 \times 6) + 8) \times 7 = 476$
There are twenty-three other possible solutions.

62

$7 - 6 + 5 - 4 = 2$
$(7 + 6 - 5) \div 4 = 2$

63

The shortest solution is eighteen moves: 2 to 3, 9 to 4, 10 to 7, 3 to 8, 4 to 2, 7 to 5, 8 to 6, 5 to 10, 6 to 9, 2 to 5, 1 to 6, 6 to 4, 5 to 3, 10 to 8, 4 to 7, 3 to 2, 8 to 1, and 7 to 10.

64

Six; two apples weigh as much as five cherries, and nine cherries weigh as much as two bananas. Thus six apples are needed to balance scale c.

65

```
  4 9 7 4 7   4 7 9 3 5 1
3 2 3   7   0   8   0   2
1   1 4 3 5 5   3 6 5 6 0 1 6
7   7   3   8   3   5   7   8
8 1 7 9   3 7 5 1 3   2 0 5 6
6   2   8   5   0   2   0   2
1 6 3 6 9 8 6   9 6 8 3 7 2 6
          5           4
2 4 6 4 0 9 3   8 7 5 7 6 2 3
1   5   5   7   2   6   2   2
8 0 6 0   3 7 2 0 6   6 7 4 2
4   9   5   8   8   3   6   0
5 8 2 9 4 6 4   7 5 2 0 0   0
      4   3   4   5   1   6 6 9
    6 8 9 0 8 3   4 6 2 0 7
```

66

```
1 9 5 1 9 7 0 9 7 5 9 1
9 7 1 7 9 5 0 1 5 7 9 9
5 0 0 9 0 9 9 0 1 1 9 1
0 9 7 5 9 7 7 9 7 0 7 7
9 5 1 9 1 5 1 0 0 5 0 0
7 9 7 0 5 7 9 9 1 7 9 9
1 1 5 7 0 1 1 0 0 5 1 5
7 7 0 9 9 5 7 0 7 9 1 7
0 0 1 5 9 9 9 5 9 1 7 1
5 7 0 0 1 0 1 7 0 9 5 7
9 9 7 0 5 9 0 7 1 5 7 0
1 1 5 9 1 7 5 9 0 7 9 1
```

67

10¼; there are two series: + 2½ and − 4¼. So we get 2¾, 5¼, 7¾, 10¼, and 13¾, 9½, 5¼.

68

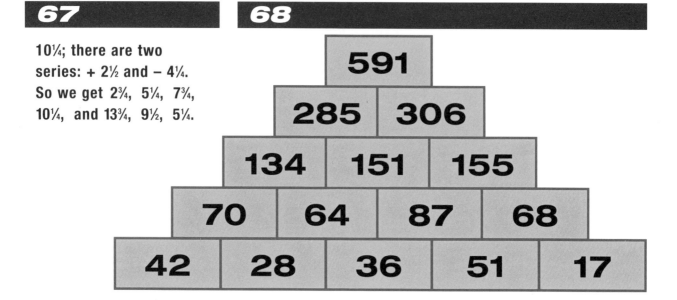

69

29; the rest are a sequence of square numbers minus 1, for example, 2² − 1 = 3, 3² − 1 = 8, 4² − 1 = 15, etc.

70

1. There are six faces to each die, which could land any way up, thus the chance of throwing a double six is one in thirty-six.

2. There are six different combinations of doubles, thus the chance of throwing any double is six in thirty-six, i.e., one in six.

3. Bearing in mind that there are two dice, the chance of throwing both a one and a six is two in thirty-six, i.e., one in eighteen.

4. With six faces to each die, the chance of throwing one particular number is eleven in thirty-six. Throwing two dice does not double your chances of throwing a four, because if you have already thrown one, the second throw is irrelevant, so in one of your six tries you don't need to throw again, i.e., only in 5/6 of the times do you add the 1/6 chance, i.e., 1/6 + 5/6 x 1/6. In other words, the chance of NOT throwing a four is 5/6 x 5/6, i.e., 25/36; thus the chance of throwing at least one four is 1 – 25/36, so 11/36.

71

J♥	K♣	A♠	Q♦
Q♠	A♦	K♥	J♣
K♦	J♠	Q♣	A♥
A♣	Q♥	J♦	K♠

72

((6 + 4) x 9 x 7) − 2 = 628

73

1. 5 and 10
2. a pair of 9s
3. 36; queen (12), king (13), and jack (11)
4. 25; 3 + 8 + 2 + queen (12), and 7 + 4 + ace (1) + king (13)
5. the 4 of clubs
6. 35; 3 + queen (12) + 9 + jack (11)

74

37

75

	9	4	1	9	4		7	0	4	1	1	8	
8	6	3		7		8		1		0		7	
6		5	8	5	2	0		3	4	9	5	0	1 2
1		7		6		5		7		6		4	4
7	2	0	6		6	6	7	5	0		2	1 8 6
0		4		4		3		2		1		5	6
3	4	5	8	2	3	2		5	8	1	9	6 7 3
		6					6						
8	7	6	1	7	1	6		2	7	5	2	1 4 6
2		1		6		7		1		4		4	4
5	5	5	9		3	2	1	3	4		8	2 8 2
1		7		9		0		8		6		9	0
8	7	4	4	9	3	4		7	2	0	5	5	0
		1		7		6		1		5		3 7 1
8	3	7	6	5	6		3	3	8	4	8		

76

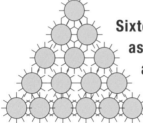

Eleven; four spades weigh as much as three hearts, and seven spades weigh as much as three diamonds. Thus eleven spades are needed to balance scale c.

77

Sixteen; six suns weigh as much as one star, and two suns weigh as much as one moon. Thus sixteen suns are needed to balance scale c.

78

1. 4,546
2. 6,534
3. 8,448
4. 10,088
5. 6,500
6. 1,234
7. 60,000
8. 8,020
9. 21,212
10. 3,136
11. 13,006
12. 9,090

79

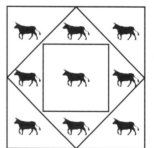

80

−19; there are two series (+19) and (−19): −76, −57, −38, and −19, −27, −46, −65.

81

		63		
	33		30	
20		13		17
13	7		6	11

82

208; the others are divisible by 19.

83

20	+	5	−	11	x	6	=	84
+		x		x		+		
6	+	20	x	5	−	11	=	119
−		+		+		x		
11	−	6	+	20	x	5	=	125
x		−		−		−		
5	x	11	+	6	−	20	=	41
=		=		=		=		
75		95		69		65		

84

Just one; its four sides run diagonally, connecting the midpoints of each side of the larger fence, just touching the corners of the smaller fence.

85

40; starting with 365, add 15 to obtain alternate numbers (so, 365, 380, 395, 410). Then, arrive at the numbers in between by multiplying the number formed by the last two digits by the first digit. So 3 x 65 = 195, and 3 x 80 = 240, etc.

86

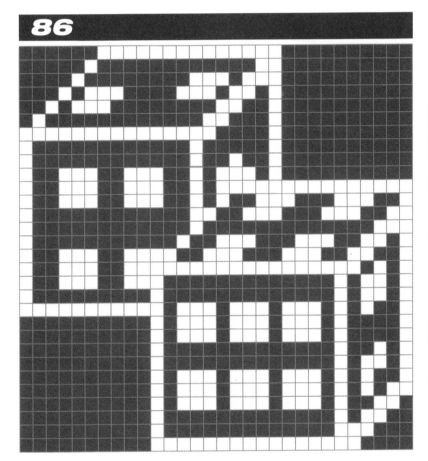

87

1:20; (start at 25 minutes past 12 o'clock, then double the number of minutes past 12 each time—i.e., 50 minutes past, 100 minutes past, 200 minutes past...)

88

((3 x 8) + 4) ÷ 2 = 14;   (3 + 8 − 4) x 2 = 14

89

12	2	15	5
1	7	10	16
13	11	6	4
8	14	3	9

90

| | | 6 | 1 | 8 | 8 | 5 | | 9 | 3 | 4 | 0 | 6 | 9 |
|8|4|7| |1| |7| |0| |5| |2| |
|7| |1|4|3|8|5| |3|1|9|9|0|2|4|
|1| |4| |2| |7| |3| |6| |8| |6|
|6|2|3|2| | |2|3|5|2|8| |3|5|8|6|
|2| |6| |8| |3| |4| |5| |1| |5|
5	0	1	8	2	0	6		4	5	0	5	9	7	9
				5						6				
9	7	2	6	7	0	8		1	3	5	3	7	4	5
1		4		5		1		3		8		0		9
5	3	5	8		7	7	5	7	6		2	7	7	9
1		5		1		1		9		7		0		5
3	1	2	9	8	1	5		9	2	5	2	8		6
	9		0		3		6		1		7	7	0
	7	8	4	5	2	9		3	8	9	2	3	

91

8	6	4	3	7	1
8	0	0	8	3	1
0	6	4	7	4	1
8	0	9	4	5	1
8	6	0	3	6	3
2	0	4	4	4	4

1. 26,973
2. 3,456
3. 3,630
4. 4,000
5. 88,088
6. 4,444
7. 13,800
8. 60,606
9. 1,111
10. 4,400
11. 1,734
12. 404

92

A maximum of fourteen (or fifteen if you include the square on which you start); there's no way of visiting the whole board, no matter which route you take.

93

37; there are twenty-one spots on each die, thus a total of sixty-three spots on the three dice. Since twenty-six spots are visible, the total number of spots on the sides that are not visible amounts to thirty-seven.

94

59

95

7,359; each number in the sequence (except the first and the odd one out) is obtained by taking the previous number and adding its two central numbers to it; e.g., 7,246 + 24 = 7,270.

96

(4 x 3) − 1 − 2 = 9
((4 + 3) ÷ 1) + 2 = 9
((4 + 3) x 1) + 2 = 9

97

98

```
2 5 2 3 5 2 5 2 5 2 5 3
5 1 3 5 2 5 2 5 3 1 5 2
3 5 2 5 1 1 5 2 5 2 5 5
2 5 5 2 5 2 1 5 1 3 2 5
2 2 5 2 5 5 3 1 2 2 5 2
1 3 1 1 2 2 2 2 5 2 2 5
5 1 5 3 2 5 1 5 3 5 2 1
1 5 2 1 5 5 3 5 2 1 1 3
5 2 1 3 2 2 5 2 1 2 3 1
5 5 1 5 5 2 5 2 1 3 1 2
2 2 3 5 1 3 5 2 5 1 5 5
5 2 1 3 2 1 2 5 2 5 1 2
```

99

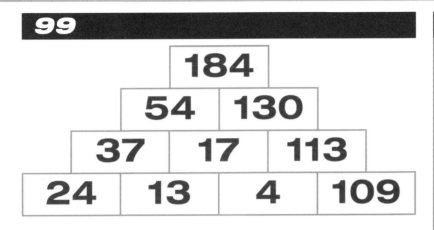

	184		
	54	130	
	37	17	113
24	13	4	109

100

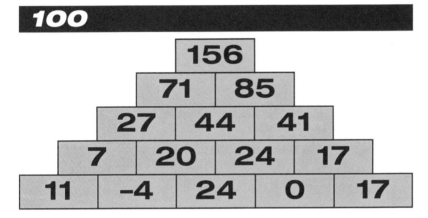

		156		
	71	85		
	27	44	41	
7	20	24	17	
11	-4	24	0	17

101

102

Each line must total twelve, thus (allowing for possible rotations and reflections) this is one possible solution:

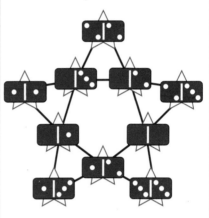

103

2,868; reverse the previous number and add 1 to the same digit each time (which starts out as the 4 of the 2,468).

104

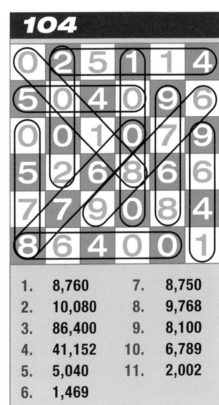

1.	8,760	7.	8,750
2.	10,080	8.	9,768
3.	86,400	9.	8,100
4.	41,152	10.	6,789
5.	5,040	11.	2,002
6.	1,469		

105

1:55; advance the previous clock by the amount shown on the clock before that; i.e., effectively add the previous two clocks together, so 1:10 and 2:05 would mean 110 plus 205, giving 315, or 3:15, the time shown on clock c, and so on.

106

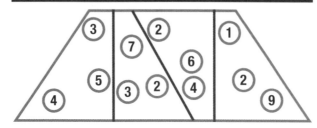

107

819; 819 is a square number followed by its square root, i.e., $9^2 = 81$, while all the other numbers are cube numbers followed by their cube roots. For example, 3,437, where $7^3 = 343$.

108

30; Angelica can see the top faces of all three dice, thus a total of fifteen spots. The opposite sides of a die add up to seven. On the furthest left die, the side face Angelica can see has one spot. On the central die, the side face Angelica can see has five spots. On the furthest right die, the side face Angelica can see has four spots. On the bottom face of the furthest right die there is one spot, so the end face of this die (invisible to you) has either two or five spots. If this end face has two spots, then the total number of spots Angelica can see is twenty-seven. But Angelica can see more spots than you, and you would be able to see twenty-nine. So the end face Angelica can see must have five spots. Thus Angelica can see a total of fifteen spots on the top faces, ten spots on the side faces, and five on the end face, so a combined total of thirty spots.

109

110

Ten routes; two clear runs and eight that go through one star.

111

15	–	4	x	9	+	14	=	113
+		x		–		+		
14	+	15	–	4	x	9	=	225
x		–		x		x		
9	x	14	+	15	–	4	=	137
–		+		+		–		
4	x	9	+	14	–	15	=	35
=		=		=		=		
257		55		89		77		

112

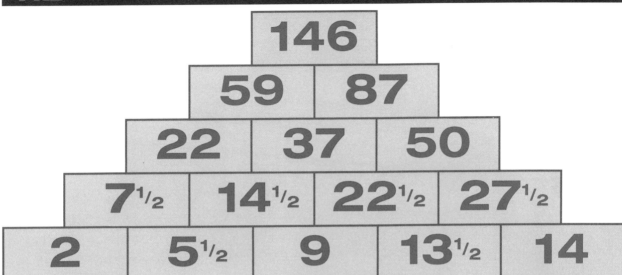

	146			
	59	87		
	22	37	50	
$7^{1/2}$	$14^{1/2}$	$22^{1/2}$	$27^{1/2}$	
2	$5^{1/2}$	9	$13^{1/2}$	14

113

4:40; in each case each hand moves forward a number of places determined by the number of letters in its last position. So, for example, the hour hand of the first clock shows one. Because this has three letters, it moves three positions to point to four on the next clock. Similarly, the minute hand of the first clock shows five, so on the next clock it shows nine because it has moved on four positions (i.e., the number of letters in five), and so on.

114

115

$((5 + 19) \div 6) \div 1 = 4$
$((5 + 19) \div 6) \times 1 = 4$

116

1. Green
2. Music 197
3. 11:15 P.M.
4. Sports 1532
5. News 350
6. Green

117

2	2	7	9	9		2	1	9	0	6	9
8	8	5		0		1		3		6		0
8		4	3	4	1	3		7	6	5	1	3	4	1
3		1		4		3		8		8		2		0
4	8	5	4		8	3	7	2	9		3	9	1	6
7		0		9		8		5		3		2		8
3	1	3	0	4	4	2		7	6	1	7	6	2	1
		0						6
6	3	5	1	9	1	5		1	1	6	6	8	7	1
8		2		6		5		5		8		2		9
5	1	9	5		7	1	3	4		8	6	3	8
2		8		6		1		1		2		5		9
9	7	1	5	9	4	4		5	2	8	4	2		5
		9		0		5		9		1		5	1	3
	7	8	7	2	6	5		6	3	2	0	7

118

(((7 x 7) − 4) x 5) x 4 = 900   There are four other possible solutions.

119

Six; one square and two circles weigh as much as one triangle; thus two squares weigh as much as one triangle, as do four circles. Therefore two circles weigh as much as one square, so we need another four circles (equivalent to two squares) plus two circles in scale c. Thus six circles are needed to balance scale c.

120

4,805; in all the others multiply the first and third digits to obtain the number formed by the second and fourth digits, for example, 4 x 5 = 20. With 4,805, multiply the second and fourth digits to obtain the number formed by the first and third digits.

121

The diagonals have no 5s, so in column 5 the second face down is a 3. In row 2, the 5 is in column 3. In column 3, the 1 is in row 4. The top right diagonal totals 23 (intro), so is 6, 3, 6, 1, 6, 1. Column 3 has a 4 in row 5 and a 6 in row 6. Column 6 has a 1 in row 3, so must have a 5 in row 4. Column 5 has a 6 in row 4. For a total of 17 (intro), the top left diagonal is (by elimination) 4, 2, 3, 4, 1, 3. Thus in row 5, column 6 is 2. Column 1 is thus 4, 6, 5, 2, 3, 1, and (by elimination) the solution is:

4	1	2	3	5	6
6	2	5	1	3	4
5	4	3	6	2	1
2	3	1	4	6	5
3	6	4	5	1	2
1	5	6	2	4	3

122

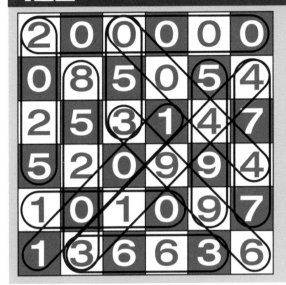

1. 31,944
2. 30,258
3. 3,996
4. 9,945
5. 2,025
6. 200,000
7. 4,400
8. 3,663
9. 1,001
10. 350
11. 1,010
12. 4,747

129

2,222; add each number to its reverse to get the next number: e.g., 605 + 506 = 1,111.

130

18; add the number of spots on the three visible faces of each die, then do the same for the invisible faces of each die. Now deduct the lower total from the higher total and multiply that answer by two.

123

One; put the smaller box inside the larger (i.e., moving the 9 coin), so the big box effectively holds all the coins.

126

(5 x ¼) − ¼ + 6 = 8¼
((5 + ½) x ¼) x 6 = 8¼

127

Note: The 9/1 tile has been inverted to become 1/6!

131

Whichever way you place the dominoes, the 0-6 is always left over.

132

63

124

1,718; to find the next number in the series, add the two middle numbers to the previous number: e.g., 1,594 + 59 = 1,653.

125

1:00; (the minute hand moves +1, +2, +3... positions forward; the hour hand is similar but moves backward instead).

128

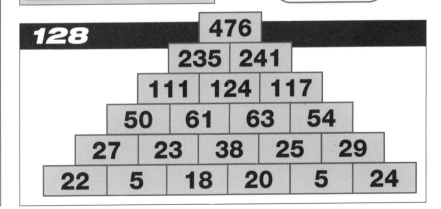

133

134

148; add all the previous digits to the last number, including the digits of the last number itself. So start with 23 + 2 + 3 = 28, and work up to 98 + 9 + 8 + 6 + 5 + 4 + 3 + 2 + 8 + 2 + 3 = 148.

135

2; in each case the hour hand moves forward one hour. The minute hand moves forward by the total given by adding the number to which the hour hand in the previous clock points to the number to which the minute hand points. So the minute hand of clock b is moved by four places (1 + 3 of clock a) to show 2:35; clock c shows 3:20 because the minute hand has moved on another nine places (2 + 7 of clock b), etc.

136

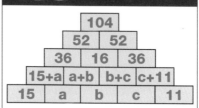

The top three levels are easy to fill in. Next, replace the three unknowns with a, b, and c. This gives us these three equations:

$36 = (15 + a) + (a + b)$
hence $2a + b = 21$

$16 = (a + b) + (b + c)$
hence $a + 2b + c = 16$

$36 = (b + c) + (c + 11)$
hence $b + 2c = 25$

Adding the first and last equation together gives $2a + 2b + 2c = 46$ hence $a + b + c = 23$

Comparing this to the middle equation shows that b must be −7, since it has another b but the total is 7 lower. Now that we know $b = -7$, it's easy to see that $a = 14$ and $c = 16$ from the other equations. The rest of the pyramid can now be completed:

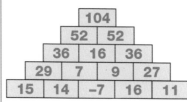

137

64; the other numbers are $4^2 - 1$, $5^2 - 1$, etc.

138

139

$((9 \times 7) + (75 \div 25)) \times (10 + 4) = 924$
There are ten other possible solutions.

140

Domino 4/0 (with the 4 at the top); the total number of dots on one domino equals the top of the domino to its right.

141

5,464; each number is obtained by taking the previous number and adding the first and last digit, i.e., 5,431 + (5 + 1 = 6) = 5,437. So 5,464 should be 5,463 for the rest of the sequence to make sense.

142

9,158; take the number formed by the odd digits in the correct order from the previous number multiplied by the number formed by the digits of the even numbers. So, 75,634 produces 753 x 64 = 48,192.

143

1. 5,040
2. 39,483
3. 9,768
4. 13,534
5. 48,400
6. 2,596
7. 9,797
8. 8,888
9. 4,400
10. 7,470
11. 38,416

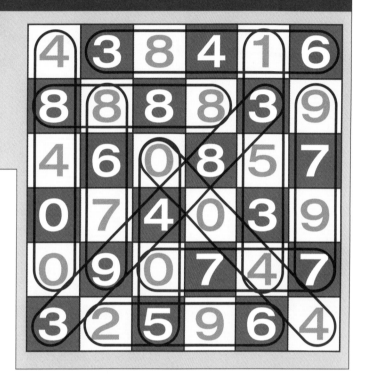

144

((24 ÷ 6) x 9) ÷ 2 = 18
((24 x 6) ÷ 9) + 2 = 18
(24 − 6 − 9) x 2 = 18

145

None; just move the tiles horizontally and vertically instead.

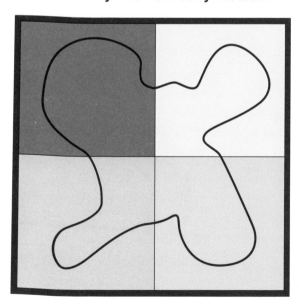

146

ACKNOWLEDGMENTS ✪ NUMBER ENIGMAS

✪ Puzzle contributors

Contributors are listed next to the numbers of the puzzles they created.

✪ David Bodycombe

Puzzles 1, 3, 5, 10, 14, 15, 17, 18, 28, 30, 31, 38, 39, 47, 53, 57, 60, 61, 62, 63, 68, 71, 72, 81, 84, 87, 88, 89, 92, 96, 99, 100, 195, 110, 112, 113, 114, 115, 118, 123, 125, 126, 127, 128, 135, 136, 139, 144, 145, 146

✪ Guy Campbell

Puzzles 6, 8, 36, 45, 59, 78, 91, 104, 122, 143

✪ Philip Carter and Ken Russell

Puzzles 16, 19, 22, 27, 29, 34, 43, 44, 48, 52, 54, 67, 69, 74, 80, 82, 85, 94, 95, 103, 107, 109, 120, 124, 129, 132, 134, 137, 141, 142

✪ Probyn Puzzles

Puzzles 2, 9, 12, 32, 55, 65, 75, 83, 90, 101, 111, 117

✪ Puzzlemakers

Puzzles 4, 7, 11, 13, 20, 21, 23, 24, 25, 26, 33, 35, 37, 40, 41, 42, 46, 49, 50, 51, 56, 58, 64, 66, 70, 73, 76, 77, 79, 86, 93, 97, 98, 102, 106, 108, 116, 119, 121, 130, 131, 133, 138, 140

Number Enigmas was commissioned, edited, designed, and produced by:

Book Creation Ltd., 20 Lochaline Street, London W6 9SH, United Kingdom

Managing Director: Hal Robinson

Editor: Alison Moore **Project Editor:** Marilyn Inglis **Art Editor:** Keith Miller

Designers: Michael Chapman, Austin Taylor; Evelyn Bercott **Copy Editor:** Sarah Barlow